CONTEMPORARY POLITICAL IDEOLOGIES
A comparative analysis

THE DORSEY SERIES IN POLITICAL SCIENCE

Consulting Editor   SAMUEL PATTERSON   University of Iowa

Contemporary political ideologies

A comparative analysis

LYMAN TOWER SARGENT
University of Missouri—St. Louis

1978 FOURTH EDITION

THE DORSEY PRESS Homewood, Illinois 60430
Irwin-Dorsey Limited Georgetown, Ontario L7G 4B3

TO EVAN

Fourth Edition

3 4 5 6 7 8 9 0 ML 5 4 3 2 1 0 9

ISBN 0-256-01993-2
Library of Congress Catalog Card No. 77–79386
Printed in the United States of America

Preface

The world today is influenced by many different views of life. Everyone has heard the names of most of them, yet when we see or hear the words communism, democracy, or nationalism we tend to react to them emotionally. We view one as good, another as bad, and seldom make the effort to understand what these words mean. This reaction is due to our acceptance, whether consciously recognized or not, of one or more of these views of life.

It is the purpose of this book to present the essential features of certain of the belief systems in the world today objectively and understandably. It is my basic assumption that an accurate, unbiased presentation of the ideas that underlie these ideologies must be a primary concern. I have attempted to avoid any encroachment of my personal opinion into the body of this work. Obviously I am not arguing that it is possible to be completely objective, but my goal is to achieve a position where the reader is allowed to suspend judgment until he or she can draw a conclusion based on accurate information.

This edition has been completely rethought, reorganized, and rewritten. Significant changes have been made in most chapters in an attempt to be more accurate, more complete, and more easily understood.

But with all the changes, the book maintains its essential character as a comparative introduction to the dominant, and some of the minor, ideologies of the modern world. In particular I have tried to maintain the usefulness and flexibility of the work as a teaching tool. It can be used as a general overview of all the ideologies, or, with the use of the updated Suggested Readings at the end of each chapter, it can be used as a means of focusing on a number of selected ideologies.

In the Suggested Readings I have tried to list the most important books plus a wide enough variety to represent most of the points of view involved. Where this is impossible, I have tried to list some bibliographies. Most of the books listed are available in paperback, but since the availability of paperback books changes rapidly, I have not tried to identify them. The student who wants to find out which ones are in paperback should consult *Paperbound Books in Print,* which can be found in any library and most bookstores.

December 1977   Lyman Tower Sargent

Contents

1

Introduction

When we go to the movies, watch television, or read the newspaper or a novel, we are being presented with a segment of the world shown from one or many angles, simple or complex, in blacks and whites, or in the many colors and shadings in between. Each of these simple actions influences the ways in which we view the world. In fact, virtually everything we do adds to our knowledge and beliefs about the world. As we grow up our family, our teachers, and our friends push and pull us in one direction or another, shaping our personality and beliefs. We also consciously choose among beliefs and attitudes, either because we weigh one position against others and judge that one is better or worse according to some standard that we have come to believe in, or perhaps simply because we respect a person who holds that belief or we want respect from that person. This whole process is very complex and the simple description here does not do it justice. But the point can be understood by noting that everything we do influences us and the way we relate to the world around us.

Gradually we come to the set of beliefs and attitudes that we will live with, that we believe represents truth whether or not we are consciously aware of it. Obviously this set of beliefs will change throughout our lives, but there will be basic beliefs that are not likely to change greatly after we reach a certain age. They may change but they are less likely to. Most of us are not deeply aware of what we believe. We don't, so to speak, take our beliefs out and examine them very often, if at all. We may rethink one position or change another without really thinking, but we rarely attempt to look carefully or thoroughly at what we believe.

In the development of our own beliefs and attitudes we are affected by a variety of belief systems, religious and/or political views of the world that are, or are at least believed to be, internally consistent and consciously held by many people—we call these beliefs ideologies. We may adopt parts of these ideologies simply because we have come to react positively or negatively to words that represent these beliefs. For example, persons growing up in the United States are likely to be certain that democracy is right and communism wrong even if they have never read a book such as this that attempts to define democracy and communism. We react to words that have emotional content even if they do not yet have intellectual content. Most people, of course, have some emotional and some intellectual content for most words.

All of us at times react on the basis of the way we have been formed by an ideology; we are at these times acting as if we held the ideology itself, even though we clearly don't hold all of the attitudes and beliefs that make up the complete ideology. On the other hand, there are people, often called ideologues, who seem to interpret all phenomena from the perspective of their ideology. Their view of the world and their answer to all questions are provided for them by their beliefs.

There is much controversy today among political scientists, sociologists, and others about the meaning and effect of ideology. I shall avoid this debate as much as possible because it seldom relates to the purpose of this book—the presentation of the major political ideologies in the modern world.[1]

The whole approach of this book assumes that ideologies do affect people and in this chapter I shall suggest a number of ways in which this takes place. I have already suggested some of these effects, even on those of us, the majority, who do not have fully developed ideologies. Imagine then, the effect on

---

[1] The reader who is interested in the current controversy over the nature of ideology should consult the Suggested Readings at the end of the chapter.

someone who *knows* that his ideology provides him with an accurate picture of the world, of the only correct relations among the members of society, and of the only right way of conducting economic and political affairs.

Having suggested in a somewhat loose way the manner in which ideology functions, I invite you to look at the concept more carefully. An ideology is a value or belief system that is accepted as fact or truth by some group. It is composed of sets of attitudes toward the various institutions and processes of society. It provides the believer with a picture of the world both as it is and as it should be, and, in so doing, it organizes the tremendous complexity of the world into something fairly simple and understandable. The degree of organization and the simplicity of the resulting picture vary considerably from ideology to ideology, and the ever-increasing complexity of the world tends to blur all the pictures, but at the same time, the basic pictures provided by the ideologies seem to remain fairly constant.

As has been indicated above, a distinction should be made between a simple belief in something and an ideology. An ideology or a belief system can be clearly distinguished from an individual's belief in something. An ideology must be a more or less connected set of beliefs that provide the believer with a fairly thorough picture of the world.[2]

In this book we will be discussing social and political ideology.[3] We will deal only with ideologies that have major and broad social and political elements and are predominately secular in nature. Adding philosophical, religious, and other beliefs that might be labeled ideological is beyond the scope of this book.

Prior to its current definition as outlined above, two major thinkers were noted for their use of the term *ideology*, Karl Marx (1818–83) and Karl Mannheim (1893–1947). Marx described as ideological any set of political *illusions* that have

---

[2] See, for example, Samuel H. Barnes, "Ideology and the Organization of Conflict: On the Relationship between Political Thought and Behavior," *Journal of Politics*, vol. 28 (August 1966), pp. 514–15.

[3] Many writers would define ideology more narrowly, for example, to *political* ideology. See Robert E. Lane, *Political Ideology: Why the American Common Man Believes What He Does* (New York: Free Press of Glencoe, 1962), pp. 14–15.

been produced by the social experience of a class. For Marx a person's membership in a particular class produces a picture of the world that is shaped by the prejudices of that class. Thus, it would be virtually impossible for an individual class member to achieve an accurate conception of the world. Marx is arguing that the socialization process (i.e., the process by which an individual incorporates the values of the society) is strongly shaped by one's place in the class or social stratification system of that society. The individual gains beliefs as a member of a class, largely because the social system requires that certain classes accept significantly different standards of living and so forth.[4]

Mannheim is close to Marx's conception, except he attempts to avoid the negative connotations that Marx intends in his definition. For Marx, ideologies are illusions that keep a class from understanding its true place in society. For Mannheim they are, in what he calls the total conception of ideology, "the characteristics and composition of the total structure of the mind" of an age or a group, such as a class.[5] This simply means what we have been saying all along; it is the set of concepts that filters the mass of information people perceive. Mannheim also uses what he calls "the particular conception of ideology" in which the belief is that the ideas of our opponents are "more or less conscious disguises of the real nature of a situation, a true recognition of which would not be in accord with his interests."[6] Again this is the belief that the other person's ideas, but not ours, are false representations of the world, an illusion or a mask, depending on whether they are consciously recognized or not.

A third writer, not normally considered in this context, deserves mention. Sigmund Freud (1856–1939) is not widely known for his relevance to the study of social phenomena.[7]

---

[4] The picture of the world provided by Marxism will be discussed further in Chapter 4.

[5] Karl Mannheim, *Ideology and Utopia: An Introduction to the Sociology of Knowledge,* trans. Louis Wirth and Edward Shils (New York: Harcourt Brace Jovanovich, 1936), p. 56.

[6] Ibid., p. 55.

[7] Freud has been the subject of two studies designed to introduce his thought to social scientists: Paul Roazen, *Freud: Political and Social Thought* (New York: Alfred A. Knopf, 1968); and Thomas Johnston, *Freud and Political Thought* (New York: Citadel Press, 1965).

For our purposes Freud makes one point about beliefs, such as ideologies, that needs to be noted. These belief systems, he argues, are usually illusions. Although these illusions are largely based on the distortion or repression of our psychological needs, they still provide an organized framework for explaining the world and its ills. An accepted explanation, even one that might be demonstrably wrong, can be comforting. Thus, Freud, like Marx, sees ideologies as illusions that keep us deluded, content with a difficult if not intolerable condition. Freud prescribes psychoanalysis if the illusion becomes sufficiently pathological; Marx prescribes revolution.

As an example of what we have been looking at so far, let us take an oversimplified and extreme case which will help both to illustrate the nature of ideology and to explain the complex process of change within it. In the past, movies presented viewers with a simple, clearly defined view of the clash of the forces of good and evil in the American West. The good guys and the bad guys were even clearly identified by white clothes and a white horse for the hero and black clothes and a black horse for the villain. The good guys always won, and the hero rode off into the sunset without any entangling alliances to keep him from his next battle with evil.

Although much of the basic pattern has not changed and the identical pattern can be found in the type of science fiction known as "space opera," many "adult" Westerns today show the two sides dressed the same and riding the same color horses. In addition, some go so far as to present the bad guy as not really bad, simply misunderstood; and the good guy as not always the epitome of all virtue. Finally, the modern hero is often attracted to women, something that never would have occurred to the earlier white-hatted hero.

These differences illustrate some of the problems in analyzing ideologies as they change over time. We shall see in some belief systems or ideologies exactly the old, rigid good–bad division. In others we shall see such a complexity of factors at work that it will be difficult or even impossible to tell the good guys from the bad guys. In these more complex ideologies, it is often found that the individual believer accepts more than one ideology. He or she accepts, for example, the positions of a political party, a church, and a business firm or labor union.

Each of these positions constitutes either a partially or a fully developed belief system or ideology, and, although certain aspects of these systems may coincide perfectly or closely enough to not cause conflict within the individual, other aspects may be widely divergent and may, if noticed, immobilize the individual because of the fundamental difference between the two beliefs held at the same time.

It should not be concluded that we all have ideologies. We all have beliefs, in large part gained from identification with or membership in some group, but, unless the beliefs are recognized or acted upon with or without recognition, it is difficult to say that we have an ideology.

There are conflicting ideologies in all societies. Assuming for the present that people select among ideological options,[8] we can, by overstating the case, illustrate the dilemma. The individual is free to pick and choose among the variety of positions that are available. Many individuals will not be aware of the wide variety of ideologies that exist, but, when they are, they may become confused, apathetic, or inactive. On the other hand, the wide variety of ideological options available within an open system tends to deemphasize ideology; the conflict within the individual, therefore, does not become as important as it would within a system in which there is only a single official ideology and the individual disagrees with that ideology.

Thus, we have the phenomenon that we noticed with the American movies of the Old West. As a society grows more and more complex, it becomes harder and harder to present a simple division between good and bad, between the white and black hats. The black and the white are mixed and become gray. We have discovered that the world is not as simple as the older movies would have us believe, and the new "adult" Western is a reflection of this recognition.

Even with this change in the pattern of some ideologies, they all attempt to organize our complex world into a pattern that will at least give some signposts to help the believer distinguish good from bad. And, finally, in all of them we shall see that the

---

[8] We must recognize that individuals do not generally choose an ideology but are brought up in such a way that they grow into their belief pattern without ever making a conscious choice.

ideal and the reality do not quite meet, and we shall witness a struggle to get them to meet through changes either in the ideal or in the reality.

In addition, within any given society, different segments of the population will hold different ideologies. For example, within the United States today, probably the overwhelming majority, if asked, would label themselves as believers in democracy. But some would call themselves anarchists, Fascists, and so forth. Every society exhibits a variety of ideologies. In no case will a given society be so completely dominated by a single ideology as to have no ideological alternatives available within the system.

Many of those who are willing to label themselves democrats and so forth do not know the meaning of the terms they use or do not act in the way the ideology would be expected to lead them. But most people build up a pattern of behavior some aspect of which comes directly from the dominant political ideology of the country in which they live. For example, if one thinks about it, it is surprising that people accept the outcome of elections rather than fighting for their side when they lose. But most people are so conditioned to accept loss in elections that they do so without ever thinking about revolt. Recent events in Lebanon and Portugal indicate that this is not always the case. Although most behavior is probably not a result of the acceptance of an ideology, some seems to be.

There are differences within each major ideology that in effect make each one a cluster of ideologies. Democracy as an ideology is perhaps the most obvious example, being composed of at least two major categories—democratic capitalism and democratic socialism. All who place themselves in either of these categories believe themselves to be democrats, and some see themselves as the only true democrats. In addition to this major division, there are numerous disagreements over the emphasis to be placed on certain aspects of democracy and over the tactics to be used in achieving the desired goals. This phenomenon is not characteristic of the democratic ideology alone but actually of all ideologies. As we know from reading the news from Eastern Europe and China in recent years, there are significant disagreements among Communists over what is essential to communism as an ideology and what is nonessential and can be changed, modified slightly, or completely discarded.

There is no ideology that is completely free from this sort of disagreement. When one speaks of a single, official ideology, it should be recognized that even these so-called single, official ideologies are not completely monolithic but are composed of a variety of factions and disagreements that go together to make up the ideology and to allow it to change to meet changing conditions.

To reiterate, individuals may hold within themselves a variety of beliefs that may be in conflict. Normally they do not recognize the conflicting nature of these beliefs, and they apply them to different situations without ever viewing their values as a whole. An interesting example of this tendency can be found in the recent history of civil rights in the United States. Christianity is usually believed to teach that all human beings should be treated equally. The segregationist who professes Christianity has historically not been consciously aware of any disparity between his or her political and religious beliefs. As many churches have come to say that segregation does not fit with Christianity, segregationists have normally responded in one of three ways. They may argue that the church should not involve itself in social or political affairs, or they may find justification within the Bible for their position, or they may gradually reject one of the two positions that appear to be in conflict.

Another example might be the person who thoroughly believes that the majority should rule, and just as thoroughly believes that for a wide variety of reasons, such as the need for secrecy in foreign affairs, that the majority cannot and should not in fact be allowed to rule in some cases. Again, either this person will fail to see the problem; or will argue that they are not irreconcilable by saying, for example, that the people actually rule, even in foreign affairs, by checking the actions of their representatives at periodic elections; or will gradually reject one of these two positions. This difficulty presents one of the most serious obstacles to a clear presentation and understanding of ideology, and it will remain a constant theme in the consideration of each ideology.

The ideologies that have been selected for consideration have been chosen on the basis of two main criteria: their importance in the world today and the desire to present the broad range of political beliefs. Nationalism, democracy, and communism clearly fall in the first category. Each one must be understood before one can intelligently grasp the news of the day. Anarchism clearly belongs in the second category. Although anarchism has never been dominant for long in any area, it still has many adherents and has a continuing popularity. A survey of political ideology would not be complete if anarchism were ignored. The others fall somewhere between these two categories. Each is important for an understanding of recent and contemporary history but not to the same degree as nationalism, democracy, and communism. In addition, each represents a point on the spectrum of political belief that is not clearly occupied by any of the others.

One, nationalism, is of a different type from all the others because it affects all the others. Nationalism is important just because it is commonly part of the other ideologies; therefore, it will be discussed first so that it will be possible to see the ways in which it affects the other ideologies.

The wide variety of different types of ideologies raises a further difficult problem for the analyst. Since each ideology is significantly different from the others, there is no single approach appropriate to all of them. The problem is that each ideology emphasizes different aspects of society and may ignore other aspects that are stressed by another ideology. Therefore, it is not possible to treat each ideology in exactly the same way. It is necessary to present the ideology as it actually is rather than as we might think an ideology should be. Thus, each one will be analyzed as its own nature dictates.

At the same time it is necessary to compare them, and, in order to do so, some way must be devised so that a similar type of information is made available for each ideology wherever possible. This will not be entirely possible because of the different emphases found in each ideology, but an effort must be made.

In order to achieve some sort of comparability, the complex of interactions among individuals, groups, and institutions that we call society has been divided into five segments:

1.   The value system.
2.   The socialization system.
3.   Social stratification and social mobility.
4.   The economic system.
5.   The political system.

This breakdown is simply a very loose set of categories designed to provide some minimal order to the analysis of ideologies. As is indicated in the following paragraphs, these categories merely allow us to describe the attitudes found in the various ideologies; they do not provide any tool for analyzing the ideologies beyond mere description.

In its simplest formulation, an ideology consists of attitudes toward the various aspects of society. For example, the democratic ideology includes the notion that all citizens should be politically equal. Of course, even the most superficial analysis of the political system in the United States, a country that accepts the democratic ideology, shows that not all citizens are politically equal. This example illustrates a number of problems that one has when discussing ideology. First, it illustrates that ideologies are not necessarily put into effect by the society. Second, a glance at the civil rights movement and the Supreme Court decisions on reapportionment may show an influence of the ideology on the social system. Third, since not all people in the United States accept this notion of political equality, it demonstrates that, within modern, complex, pluralistic societies, there are a number of significantly different competing value systems that must be considered.

Any analysis of any part of society, including the value system, is an attempt to answer a series of questions regarding the various institutions and processes mentioned above. This series of questions can be divided into two parts: (1) How should society function; and (2) how does society in fact function? The answers to the first question give us a picture of the value system. The answers to the second question give us an image of the social system in operation.

Below is a set of questions designed to provide a fairly complete analysis of the assumptions of a political ideology. By using questions like these, one is able to compare the ideologies.

I.   Human nature.
    A.   What are the basic characteristics of human beings as human beings?
    B.   What effect does human nature have upon the political system?
II. The origin of society and government or the state.

     A.   What is the origin of society? Why does it develop?

     B.   What is the origin of government or the state? Why does it develop?

III.   Political obligation (duty, responsibility, law).

     A.   Why do people obey the government?

     B.   Why should people obey the government, or should they obey it at all?

     C.   Is disobedience ever justifiable?

     D.   Is revolution ever justifiable?

IV.   Freedom and liberty (rights—substantive and procedural).

     A.   Are men and women free in any way vis-à-vis the government?

     B.   Should they be free vis-à-vis the government?

     C.   Assuming that some type, or types, of freedom are both possible and desirable, what should these be? Should they be limited or unlimited? Who places the limits?

V.   Equality.

     A.   Are individuals in any way "naturally" equal?

     B.   Should they be in any way equal?

     C.   Assuming that some type, or types, of equality are both possible and desirable, what should these be? Should they be absolute or relative? If relative, what criteria should be used to establish them? Who establishes the criteria? Who enforces the criteria?

VI.   Community (fraternity).

     A.   Should ties among individuals composing a group form a bond that takes precedence over the needs and wishes of the individual members of the group?

     B.   If this is desirable, how can it be encouraged? If this is undesirable, how can it be discouraged? Who decides?

VII.   Power (authority).

     A.   Should any individual or group of individuals be able to control, determine, or direct the actions of others?

     B.   If this is desirable, what form or forms should it take? Should it be limited or unlimited? Who limits and how?

VIII.   Justice.
    A.   It is usually assumed that justice is desirable, but what is it? Is it individual or social?
    B.   Who decides the characteristics of justice? Who enforces these characteristics?
  IX.   The end of society or government.
    A.   For what purposes does society or government exist?
    B.   Who decides these purposes or are they consciously chosen?
   X.   Structural characteristics of government.
    A.   What is the best or best possible form of government? Why?
    B.   Are there alternative forms of government that are equally valid? What is the standard of judgment? Who decides?

From the viewpoint of the study of ideology, the value system of a society is its most important characteristic. In some ways, the value system *is* the ideology. But it should be kept in mind that unless one speaks of value systems rather than a value system, one is likely to radically oversimplify one's analysis. There is seldom one completely dominant value system or ideology within any given society. It is most appropriate, therefore, to speak of the value system as being made up of subsystems. In order to understand these ideologies, and particularly their value systems, we must comprehend the theoretical or philosophical basis of them. Much of each of the analyses of the ideologies will, therefore, be necessarily given over to a commentary on questions generally regarded as part of political philosophy.[9] In addition, each chapter will attempt to give some idea of the attitudes toward the various institutions and processes of society found in each ideology. It will be possible to see what questions are important to each ideology, and thus some basis will be established for comparing them.

Before this can be done, it will be necessary to understand a bit more about each of these institutions and processes. The

---

[9] Loosely, political philosophy aims at an understanding of political values and norms. Political ideology is a value or belief system that is accepted as being correct.

socialization system is probably the most important segment of society. It is the process by which individuals gain the values of the society as their own. It is generally assumed that the most important institutions that affect the ways in which, and the degree to which, the individual gains these values are (1) the family system, (2) the educational system, (3) the religious system, and (4) a variety of other influences such as the mass media, the peer group, and so forth. We are not always sure of the mechanism by which the various institutions of socialization operate. It is, of course, fairly obvious that a child is strongly influenced in his or her whole outlook on life by family environment and at least by early school years. It is perhaps less clear how the other institutions of socialization influence an individual's outlook on life. We can perhaps assume that the same messages repeated over and over again in institutions that the individual has been taught to respect, such as the religious and educational systems, may have a cumulative effect and thus ultimately become part of the individual's value system. The mass media probably operates in the same way.

The social stratification system is the way in which the society ranks individuals within it. This ranking may be a very clearly defined class system or it may be very loose, with the lines between classes or status groups somewhat hazy. Social stratification is usually summed up within a political ideology by the question of equality. Some ideologies contain the idea that everyone within the society should be equal in specified ways. For example, some people talk about equality of opportunity and political equality; others believe in economic and social equality. Only if there were no economic, social, political, or any other inequalities would there be no social stratification system. Almost no one has ever suggested such complete equality, but each of these more limited types of equality has been suggested or tried at various times and will be discussed later.

One of these types of equality, equality of opportunity, is particularly important in any society. Equality of opportunity means that no artificial obstacles or barriers should keep any individual or group from moving from one class to another if they have the ability. Equality of opportunity defines certain parts of the social mobility system within a society. Every society has such a mobility system which determines the ease or difficulty with which an individual can move among classes or statuses in the society. The system also determines the basis for such movement. For example, in traditional China an individual could move into the upper classes of the society by successfully completing a series of examinations. Many contemporary societies have no such formal system but base mobility on such standards as wealth.

The economic system is concerned with the production, distribution, and consumption of wealth. The major parts of the economic system that will concern us relate to (1) production, (2) distribution and consumption, and (3) the relationship of the economic system to the political system. We shall be particularly concerned with questions concerning the degree of economic equality desired by the ideology and the means that the ideology sets for achieving this goal. Since most ideologies reject extremes of wealth and poverty that are too great, they have developed means of correcting the imbalance such as, for example, the graduated income tax or the nationalization of industries.

Most of the economic questions that we will discuss deal with more purely political questions. The political system is that segment of society that draws together or integrates all the others. The political system can make decisions that are binding upon the whole society, and thus it holds the key to any understanding of the whole ideological and social system. To some degree, a political ideology includes all of the above questions in one form or another.

SUGGESTED READINGS

A good bibliography on the question of ideology can be found on pp. 369–73 of the volume edited by Richard H. Cox listed below.

Apter, David E., ed. *Ideology and Discontent.* New York: Free Press, 1964.

Barnes, Samuel H. "Ideology and the Organization of Conflict: On the Relationship between Political Thought and Behavior," *Journal of Politics,* vol. 28 (August 1966), pp. 513–30.

Benewick, Robert; Berki, R. N.; and Parekh, Bhikhu, eds. *Knowledge and Belief in Politics; The Problem of Ideology.* London: George Allen & Unwin, 1973.

Bergmann, Gustave. "Ideology," *Ethics,* vol. 61 (April 1951), pp. 205–18.

Bluhm, William T. *Ideologies and Attitudes; Modern Political Culture.* Englewood Cliffs, N.J.: Prentice–Hall, 1974.

Brown, L. B. *Ideology.* Harmondsworth: Penguin, 1973.

Christenson, Reo M. et al. *Ideologies and Modern Politics.* New York: Dodd, Mead & Co., 1971.

Connolly, William E. *Political Science & Ideology.* New York: Atherton Press, 1967.

Corbett, Patrick. *Ideologies.* London: Hutchinson, 1965.

Cox, Richard H., ed. *Ideology, Politics, and Political Theory.* Belmont, Calif.: Wadsworth Publishing Co., 1969.

Drucker, H. M. *The Political Uses of Ideology.* London: Macmillan & Co., 1974.

Germino, Dante. *Beyond Ideology: The Revival of Political Theory,* Parts I and II. New York: Harper & Row, 1967.

Gross, Felike, ed. *European Ideologies; a Survey of 20th Century Political Ideas.* Freeport, N.Y.: Books for Libraries Press, 1971. Originally published in 1948.

Gyorgy, Andrew, and Blackwood, George D. *Ideologies in World Affairs.* Waltham, Mass.: Blaisdell Publishing Co., 1967.

Halle, Louis J. *The Ideological Imagination.* Chicago: Quadrangle Books, 1972.

Huntington, Samuel P. "Conservatism as an Ideology," *American Political Science Review,* vol. 51 (June 1957), pp. 454–73.

Kohn, Hans. *Political Ideologies of the 20th Century.* 3d ed. rev. New York: Harper & Row, 1966.

Lane, Robert E. *Political Ideology: Why the American Common Man Believes What He Does.* New York: Free Press of Glencoe, 1962.

Lichtheim, George. *The Concept of Ideology and Other Essays.* New York: Random House, 1967.

McClosky, Herbert. "Consensus and Ideology in American Politics," *American Political Science Review,* vol. 58 (June 1964), pp. 366–82.

Mannheim, Karl. *Ideology and Utopia: An Introduction to the Sociology of Knowledge.* Trans. Louis Wirth and Edward Shils. New York: Harcourt Brace Jovanovich, 1936.

Mullins, Willard A. "On the Concept of Ideology in Political Science," *American Political Science Review,* vol. 66 (June 1972), pp. 498–510.

Plamenatz, John. *Ideology.* London: Pall Mall, 1970.

Preston, Nathaniel Stone. *Politics, Economics, and Power; Ideology and Practice under Capitalism, Socialism, and Fascism.* New York: Macmillan Co., 1967.

Rejai, Mostafa, ed.   *Decline of Ideology?* Chicago: Aldine–Atherton, 1971.

————; Wilson, W. L.; and Beller, D. C.   "Political Ideology: Empirical Relevance of the Hypothesis of Decline," *Ethics,* vol. 78 (July 1968), pp. 303–12.

Seliger, Martin.   *Ideology and Politics.* New York: Free Press, 1976.

Shklar, Judith N., ed.   *Political Theory and Ideology.* New York: Macmillan Co., 1966.

2

Nationalism

The word *nationalism* is in constant use today, usually in connection with a war or revolution. In North American newspapers, it is used with reference to the countries of Africa, Asia, Latin America, or the Middle East. And, in addition, *nationalism* is used to describe minority movements within countries, such as the Black Nationalists in the United States, the Basques in Spain, and the French-Canadian Separatists in Canada. We seldom think of ourselves as nationalists. If we think in these terms at all, we view ourselves as being patriotic. But the words *nationalism* or *patriotism* are rarely precisely defined. Nationalism is generally thought of as something bad, and patriotism as something good. The good American may be called patriotic, but not nationalistic. It takes only a little reflection to recognize that they represent similar phenomena. Therefore, *nationalism* and *patriotism* must be carefully defined and consistently used as defined.

Nationalism is an ideology of an unusual sort in that it affects all other ideologies. All ideologies, even anarchism, have been tinged by nationalism from time to time, and currently it is fair to say that all ideologies are now constantly affected by nationalism. And thus nationalism may be the most important of the ideologies.

Therefore, in defining *nationalism* and *patriotism,* we will be defining key elements of all the ideologies. And, in order to be complete we must also look at the rejection of nationalism through the acceptance of what we can label *internationalism*. Although there are few people who view the whole world in the same way, with the same love that they view their own country, there are some who do and more who believe they should and attempt to do so. On the face of it, internationalism may seem to be a very different kind of phenomenon from nationalism. Without overdoing the analogy, we can compare the difference to the differing, but strong, feelings a person may have toward, for example, the state of Florida and the United States. Most American citizens do have some sense of loyalty toward both their home state and the United States. Many do not have a sense of loyalty to the world as a whole, but this is not to say that the feelings of those who do are essentially different from a person who feels strongly about both Florida and the United States. Internationalism is the same type of phenomenon as patriotism and nationalism, and perhaps by looking at all three, we shall be able to understand each one more thoroughly.

The problem of definition is central here. Nationalism was first brought to the attention of most people either by World War I and the question of national self-determination, by the rise of fascism and national socialism and World War II, or by the many recent wars and revolutions conducted in the name of nationalism and anticolonialism. It has been kept constantly in the news by the continuing breakup of colonialism in Latin America, Asia, and Africa, enhanced by the troubles in Vietnam and the Middle East. Nationalism, therefore, is equated with trouble and probably could not have been kept free from its negative connotations. Patriotism, at least in the United States, has a somewhat more positive tone to it. But it also refers to the so-called 100 percent American, the one who is so patriotic that he cannot see anything good anywhere else in the world. Thus, patriotism sometimes means an unrealistic isolation and unreasoning devotion to country. *Internationalism* is the most neutral of the three terms since there are so few examples of internationalists that the word has few emotional overtones.

The ability to understand the feeling or conviction that is nationalism is limited by one's inability to express adequately such a feeling. Still, some attempt must be made. Symbols of nationality such as the flag and the national anthem are supposed to produce in one a feeling akin to patriotism. It is probably true that even the most unnationalistic of us has, in fact, felt the effect of such symbols at one time or another. The effect is hard to characterize. Perhaps it is a thrill of recognition at belonging to something larger and more important than ourselves. Perhaps it is simply the feeling of belonging. Phrased another way, it might be the recognition that our destinies and our lives are wrapped up in the destinies and lives of many others. But our recognition of this comes through symbols. We cannot see in others the same thing that we can see and feel in a symbol. We respond to it emotionally; we do not think about what a poor piece of music the national anthem may be or that the flag is simply different colored cloth sewn together. We see in it and feel in it an emotion that makes us one with a community.

In this way, nationalism can act upon an individual more powerfully than any other ideology. All ideologies can affect individuals emotionally, and each ideology has certain sacred symbols that produce a reaction in the believer. But nationalism is stronger than any of these others because the symbols and signs produce the reaction sometimes even in the nonbeliever who has been conditioned from birth to react emotionally to flag, country, national anthem, and so forth. It seems to affect individuals more deeply and needs less reinforcement than do any of the other ideologies. Individuals often can gain a deep commitment to a nation that cannot be changed easily. The other ideologies may become this deeply rooted within an individual, but they seem to do so less often.

The feelings that nationalism arouse have been presented and defended in many ways. Teutonic or German nationalism reached heights of emotion in the operas of Richard Wagner.[1] They appeal to, and they are built upon, deeply held feeling. In the same way, but on a less emotional level, Edmund Burke appeals to this feeling as he talks about society as a pact between those living, those dead, and those yet to be born.[2] It is, for Burke, a union among all generations that cannot be lightly

---

[1] Wilhelm Richard Wagner (1813–83) is best known for his operas expressing German mythology.

[2] Edmund Burke (1729–97), a famous British politician and political philosopher, who is primarily remembered as a founder of modern conservatism. See his *Reflections on the Revolution in France*, ed. Thomas H. D. Mahoney (Indianapolis, Ind.: Bobbs-Merrill Co., 1955), p. 110.

changed or broken. The nation is something, for Burke, that is for all eternity. Wagner is more emotional, and he presents in his operas the basic folk tales and myths that, to him, are the rudiments and the roots of a great German nation. Therefore, it is not surprising that Adolf Hitler, who in *Mein Kampf* expresses such great feeling for the German nation, was a great lover of the operas of Wagner. Hitler built national socialism on the same basic feelings and some of the same ideas that Wagner presented musically.[3]

There are a few words, such as *nationalism,* that are concerned with a variety of ties or connections among individuals that somehow form a new entity; for example, such words and phrases as *community* and *public* or *national interest.* We can see this process in operation in a small, intimate group of individuals, such as the family, which is made up of individuals with different interests and, to some extent, different outlooks on life, but with a common factor that helps them to form a unit. The family continues over generations and has an emotional unity which provides a basis for identification. But there is a considerable difference between the ties of a family and something as distant or abstract as a nation or the public. Nevertheless, there is at least one fundamental similarity: the recognition of both the family and the nation as an entity presupposes some sort of recognition of groups of people forming something lasting that is more than its parts.

Part of the problem here is found in the English language. It makes it difficult for us to speak of group identity without using hybrid terms. For example, when we speak of national interest, we probably want to imply that the nation is something separate from, and perhaps more than, the sum of the individuals that compose it. We can say that we are conscious of, or recognize, the nation or the public, but the words do not have the emotional content that make it possible to readily express a feeling of unity or identity.

An additional problem is found in the fact that people vary in the extent to which they feel this group consciousness. Some people may not feel it at all. Some identify completely with a

---

[3] In the later chapters, we will discuss the ideas of a variety of nationalists. Here we will present the general concept.

group. The latter seldom think of themselves as anything but a member of a particular group. Still, we have a difficult time expressing this feeling because the language does not provide us with the appropriate words. There is no phrase in English that can really evoke the feeling of group unity or identity.

In considering the problem of definition in this way, we have not simply confused the issue but have, instead, discovered an important key to the analysis of nationalism as an ideology. All of the words and phrases considered relate to ties or links among individuals that go to form a new entity with which the individuals can identify and toward which they can have feelings of loyalty. In nationalism, this entity is the nation or the nationality. But again the words *nation* and *nationality* are imprecise. Again it is difficult to know exactly what they mean. What is a nation? What is a nationality? Are they different from a state? From a country? Can there be more than one nationality within a nation? What is it that provides the ties that go to make up these entities?

These questions cannot all be answered here, but there are workable definitions for *patriotism* and *nationalism,* as given by Leonard W. Doob:

> *Patriotism:*   the more or less conscious conviction of people that their own welfare and that of the significant groups to which they belong are dependent upon the preservation or expansion (or both) of the power and culture of their society.
> *Nationalism:*   the set of more or less uniform demands (1) which people in a society share, (2) which arise from their patriotism, (3) for which justifications exist and can be readily expressed, (4) which incline them to make personal sacrifices in behalf of their government's aims, and (5) which may or may not lead to appropriate action.[4]

Obviously, for Doob, patriotism is the basic phenomenon with nationalism as a possible product. Hence, it would appear that patriotism, as defined above, is a necessary prerequisite for the development of nationalism.

In explaining his definitions, Doob goes on to point out that patriotism as he has defined it is probably universal, but that nationalism is probably not because the demands are not al-

---

[4] Leonard W. Doob, *Patriotism and Nationalism: Their Psychological Foundations* (New Haven, Conn.: Yale University Press, 1964), p. 6.

ways present. It is always possible for patriotism to give rise to nationalism, particularly if the individual believes that his or her society is threatened. Finally, Doob says that both definitions are not historically limited, so that they refer to patriotism or nationalism at any time or place.[5] This is the type of definition that is necessary for a thorough understanding of nationalism.

Let us now examine Doob's definition more carefully. First, patriotism stripped of all its connotations comes down to a person's belief that his or her best interests are served by "the preservation or expansion (or both) of the power and culture of his society." Nationalism is sometimes popularly supposed to relate primarily to the expansion of the power of a society, but a brief glimpse at any case of nationalism will illustrate Doob's point. For example, the nationalism attributed to the developing countries is clearly not only a nationalism of power but also one of culture. Italian nationalism under Benito Mussolini was distinctly concerned with both power and culture. For Mussolini, it was the greatness of Rome that provided his goal, and it was not only the vast territories that Rome had controlled that interested Mussolini but also the intellectual and cultural leadership it had exercised. Virtually all countries do the same thing. All these cases illustrate the basic feeling of patriotism that gives rise to nationalism. The demands that Doob calls nationalism have the five characteristics outlined in the definition. They must be shared, based on patriotism, have some justification that is valid to the individuals involved, produce the possibility of personal sacrifice, and lead to actions on the part of the individuals to bring about the desired goals.

Nationalism defined, it is appropriate to look at internationalism, which we indicated earlier could be considered similar to nationalism. Immediately, one notices that it does not usually produce the same emotional fervor as does nationalism. Internationalism seems to be something of the reason rather than the emotions. People who support internationalism argue against the feelings aroused by nationalism, saying that they are divisive in their impact and that they lead to innumerable dangerous confrontations between nations. Internationalists believe that the world as a whole should be in some way united. They do

---

[5] Ibid., pp. 6–7.

not all agree on what this way should be. Some, for example, argue for a world government with very strong powers. Others argue for some sort of loose confederation, and still others argue for a federal system of government similar to that of the United States, where powers would be divided between a world government and the government of each country making up the world government.

In a general sense, internationalism does partake of the same sort of phenomena that nationalism does. It requires a recognition of ties among all individuals in the world in the same sense that nationalism requires a recognition of ties among the others that live in a particular country. We noted the symbols that give rise to the feeling of nationalism. Internationalism does not have such symbols, and it is likely that an individual will seldom have an emotional identification with the world as a whole, even though he or she may intellectually recognize his or her ties to others around the world. Thus, internationalism is not likely to be as strong a force in the 20th century as nationalism is unless some crisis produces the need for these ties to be recognized and the emotional fervor that would bring about an actual identification of the individual with a world community.

Finally, it might be useful to make a few general comments about the political implications of nationalism in today's world. The most obvious political effect of nationalism is divisiveness in the international community. We see this in Eastern Europe, where various countries have attempted, with some success, to overcome the domination of the Soviet Union, in the split within the Common Market over agricultural policy and in the disagreement between the Common Market and the United States over oil policy. The second effect of nationalism, which can be seen as a second level of divisiveness, is found in the emerging nations of Africa, Asia, and the Middle East. These nations have recognized some of the advantages of unity among themselves, but nationalism has made it impossible for them to work effectively together. In addition, feelings of nationalism have put wedges between the newly emerging nations and the older colonial powers. But, of course, nationalism has also provided a means of unifying countries. The rejection of the colonial power by the emerging nation often acts as a means of developing a national identity, cohesiveness, and purpose.

It is a common argument among some scholars of international politics that to some extent nationalism affects virtually all acts of a country in its dealings with other countries. Each country defines what is in its national interest and attempts to act as a separate unit in achieving this desired goal. Only when alliances are viewed as serving this national interest will these countries join together with others.

Nationalism is a central concern of the developing nations because in many cases they are literally new nations with which the people have no identification. Even in those nations that are at least similar in territory and have a long-standing identification as a unit, such as India, a variety of loyalties, such as caste or language, adversely affect attempts to solve or even identify national problems. In many of the new African countries, tribal loyalties have been historically more important than national loyalties, and in some cases tribal boundaries are not coterminous with national ones. In such cases there is a deep-rooted problem of conflicting loyalties that will cause serious difficulties for many years. The problem of conflicting loyalties connected with the desire on the part of political leaders to develop a loyalty and identification with the nation is undoubtedly one of the most serious problems for the new nations. It is clear that there is no simple solution, and it is difficult to know how to develop an identification with the nation, while not destroying the identification with tribal units, for example. This is particularly a problem when the tribal units cross national boundaries.

The significance of nationalism in the ideologies of the developing nations, even, or perhaps particularly, where it is not reflected in the feelings of the people, cannot be ignored. Some scholars have used the term *nation-building*[6] almost as an equivalent to modernization. The point is a simple one. Can a nation exist very long and thus achieve modernization unless its citizens identify with it? How can a government solve problems unless the people view themselves as part of a unit? How do you manufacture a tradition and an identification? These questions are simple to pose, but they do not lend themselves to simple

---

[6] See, for example, Karl W. Deutsch and William J. Foltz, eds., *Nation-Building* (New York: Atherton Press, 1963).

solutions. These problems are not solved with the regalia of a nation, a flag, an anthem, a great seal, an army, and so on, but all these things may help.

Japan is an interesting case of the problems and forces involved. Japan had a long tradition of rule by one family, but it had almost always actually been ruled by someone other than the emperor. In the 19th century, Japanese scholars rediscovered the historical role of the emperor as a strong ruler. This discovery, combined with a rediscovery of the traditional culture, helped pave the way for a revolution to give back to the emperor the powers he had once held. The emperor was technically given back his power, but actually the tradition of dualistic rule was maintained. At the same time, the revolution helped develop a reidentification with Japan on the part of many people. The fact that this was one of the forces that ultimately led to fascism and the war in the Pacific should give one pause with regard to the development of nationalism in the new African and Asian countries.[7]

One of the major difficulties facing these nations in molding an identity is the lack of knowledge of their histories and cultures. In African countries, for example, often the histories or cultures that are known are tribal, not national, and therefore they serve as only a partial solution. These tribal cultures, some of which are highly developed and in some cases very sophisticated, were also political entities in some instances. The new nations sometimes simply cut across these tribal boundaries and split up a people with an identification and included within the national boundaries people without an identification with each other or with the nation. Although some of the tribal cultures and tribal identification are of recent origin, they provide a focus of loyalty that is separate from national loyalty. This fact complicates the efforts to create a national identity and tradition.

---

[7] In his book *The Ideology of Fascism; the Rationale of Totalitarianism,* A. James Gregor calls fascism "the first revolutionary mass movement regime which aspired to commit the totality of human and natural resources of an historic community to national development" (New York: Free Press, 1969), p. xii. Hence the parallels between fascism and some of the recent modernization movements are probably not accidental. But, for a counter argument, see Arnold Hughes and Martin Kolinsky, " 'Paradigmatic Fascism' and Modernization: A Critique," *Political Studies,* vol. 24 (December 1976), pp. 371–96.

Unfortunately for these countries, a national tradition cannot be manufactured overnight; but there is at least one factor that can be used to help develop a national identity—the colonial experience. In addition, the movement to rid the country of the colonial power usually is a nationalist movement and helps to form some identity. This does not suffice, of course, to maintain an identity after the movement has succeeded. It is clear that the colonial experience does provide some ties among the developing nations, but these ties are not deep-rooted because the colonial experiences were significantly different from country to country. The nationalist movement may also help to tie a particular nation together for awhile, but such a movement cannot last indefinitely. India is an example of a one-party dominant political system based on a nationalist movement which is today, about 30 years after independence, losing its political unity and having to make the adjustment to the diversity that the nationalist movement and the Congress party helped to put off for a time. Other countries will go through the same experience of having the nationalist movement hold the country together for a time, but not indefinitely.

A brief glance at the definition of nationalism will illustrate the complexity of the problem. First, an individual must believe that "his own welfare and that of the significant groups to which he belongs are dependent upon the preservation or expansion (or both) of the power and culture of his society." Second, one must share a set of demands with others in his or her society which one believes to be justified and which incline one to personal sacrifice. The first point is the most problematic in the setting of the developing nations, but the development of a shared set of demands is almost equally difficult. Here again, we have the problem of identification with a group that simply does not exist in many of these new nations. It is problematical if such identification can be easily created. The United States was in many ways the first new nation that did succeed in developing national identity and loyalty.[8] In addition, many South American countries have seemingly succeeded in establishing some sort of identity in the minds of their people, but they are beset with all the other problems that the new nations of Africa and Asia

---

[8] See Seymour M. Lipset, *First New Nation: The United States in Historical and Comparative Perspective* (New York: Basic Books, 1963).

have. Therefore, it is clear that national identity is not necessarily the solution to the problem even if one can achieve it.

Obviously, the first prerequisite was or is national independence. There is a general division into two camps among the ideologies. One group contends that revolution is the only means of achieving independence; the other argues that reform or evolution is the best approach and that it is a possible approach in most, but not all, colonial areas.

The problem of revolution at the time of independence is more complicated than one might think. In the first place, a revolution can at times achieve a form of national unity; it can tie people together in a common effort and give them some sort of feeling for the country as a whole. At the same time, a revolution can be extremely destructive of whatever economic development the nation has achieved under the colonial rulers. A revolution is likely to destroy those things that the country needs immediately after independence. Therefore, in this sense, revolution is clearly a two-edged sword. It may help form national loyalties while at the same time destroying the possibility of rapid economic development or even economic independence. The evolutionary side of the argument has similar problems, but from the other angle. A gradual change toward independence has seemingly immense advantages. In the first place, the colonial power may help train individuals to take over the civil service and industrial positions that are so important for any country. The tools of economic development, the industries, the plantations, and so forth, are also unlikely to be destroyed. At the same time, though, this gradual change is first and foremost gradual. It does not provide for meeting the desires of the people to be free *today*. It asks them to put off their freedom until some future date. It asks them to deny themselves this goal for a time. It is also not as likely to produce any feeling of national unity or loyalty.

After formal independence is achieved, there is the problem of economic ties with the excolonial power that may constitute continuance of control. This is known as *neocolonialism*. Again, there is a revolution–evolution split in the ideologies, but most of the new countries seem able to develop some sort of rapprochement with the former colonists, usually to mutual advantage. The problem of neocolonialism is a complex one. It is clearly essential for rapid economic development that the new nation be able to trade with older, more established nations. Very often the only thing that the new nation has to trade is raw materials. The colonial power most often exploited the nation by taking out its raw materials and giving little or nothing in exchange. It is hard for the leaders of the new nation to see their raw materials going to a more highly developed country, even though they are getting something in return such as manufactured goods or even industries. Therefore, many of these new nations have insisted that the processing of the raw materials they sell must take place in the country, thus producing an industry, employing people, and giving them some sense that they are not being exploited. The problem stems in large part from the fact that raw materials sell on the world market at a much lower price than do manufactured goods. Therefore, the new nation feels that it is being exploited by selling a commodity that is relatively inexpensive in order to purchase one that is relatively expensive. The people believe that they are losing.

The same thing is often true of farmers in the United States today. They argue that what they produce and are paid for sells very cheaply, but that what they have to buy in order to live is very expensive. Consequently, they feel that they are being exploited and cheated. Such attitudes make neocolonialism an extremely important and difficult issue for the new nation. It must deal with older, more developed countries, often including its previous colonial ruler, in order to survive, but it feels that it is being exploited in virtually the same way it was while it was still a colony. The difficulty of the situation is greatly enhanced when the former colonial power is one of the neocolonial powers because there are certain identifications in the mind of the people and particularly in the nationalist leaders that make it difficult for them to view the old rulers objectively and deal with them solely in economic terms. Still, some sort of arrangement is necessary which will provide each side with the economic goods that they require while avoiding this neocolonialist label. This problem has not been solved as yet.

A third part of contemporary nationalism has been noted already, the attempt to develop or revive an indigenous culture.[9] The attempt to revitalize indigenous cultures is characteristic of

---

[9] Black Nationalism in the United States is faced with a similar problem—how to develop a black culture as a basis for the nationalist movement.

most of the new nations, but it can pose serious problems when certain traditions or aspects of the culture impede develop- ment. In India, for example, caste works against cooperation across caste lines, religious proscriptions stand in the way of an adequate diet, and language differences fragment the society as a whole. Thus, a concern for culture and tradition can both help and impede the process of modernization. We do not know enough about the particular traditional cultures of Africa to be able to say much about the extent to which these cultures im- pede or help industrialization. It has been contended that the religious system of Puritanism helped greatly in the develop- ment of capitalism and hence industrialization in the United States.[10] Likewise, there may be elements of the religious sys- tems of Africa and Asia that will either help or impede indus- trialization. We simply do not as yet know enough about the situations to say.

Two other patterns, both in the process of change, need to be mentioned: regionalism and nonalignment. The developing countries have, with the exception of the Latin American coun- tries, who may not be free to choose, attempted to avoid align- ing themselves with any side in the various disagreements among the major powers of the world. And the Latin American countries are beginning to follow this pattern. At the same time, they have attempted to form regional coalitions to help solve common problems and to present a united front to the world. Regionalism, though, is of growing importance. Although the attempts to join two or more countries together have generally failed, loose regional coalitions have provided a forum for the consideration of common problems and have led to some co- operation. But regionalism will not develop into confederation or federation as long as the dominant theme is nationalism.

We have previously discussed the impact of nationalism on the individual nationalist, but it would still be appropriate to reiterate the point briefly. The individual is emotionally affected by nationalism. This can influence him in all his perceptions of the world and of the various peoples in it. Although it can unite the individuals within a country, nationalism can separate them from individuals in other countries.

---

[10] See Max Weber, The Protestant Ethic and the Spirit of Capitalism, trans. Talcott Parsons (New York: Charles Scribner's Sons, 1930).

SUGGESTED READINGS

Since two bibliographies on nationalism are available, the following list is composed of general works. Some further works relating nationalism to particular political ideologies may be found in the Suggested Readings following the other chapters.

Bibliographies

Deutsch, Karl W.   *Interdisciplinary Bibliography on Nationalism 1935–1953*. Cambridge, Mass.: Technology Press, 1955.

Pinson, Koppel S.   *A Bibliographic Introduction to Nationalism*. New York: Columbia University Press, 1935.

General works

Akzin, Benjamin.   *State and Nation*. London: Hutchinson University Library, 1964.

———, ed.   *Nationalism in Asia and Africa*. New York: Meridian Books, 1970.

Baron, Salo W.   *Modern Nationalism and Religion*. New York: Harper & Row, 1947.

Carr, Edward Hallett.   *Nationalism and After*. London: Macmillan & Co., 1945.

Chadwick, ·H. Munro.   *The Nationalities of Europe and the Growth of National Ideologies*. Cambridge, Eng.: Cambridge University Press, 1945.

Deutsch, Karl W.   *Nationalism and Social Communication: An Inquiry into the Foundations of Nationality*. 2d ed. Cambridge, Mass.: M.I.T. Press, 1966.

———.   *Nationalism and Its Alternatives*. New York: Alfred A. Knopf, 1969.

———, and Foltz, William J., eds.   *Nation-Building*. New York: Atherton Press, 1963.

Doob, Leonard W.   *Patriotism and Nationalism: Their Psychological Foundations*. New Haven, Conn.: Yale University Press, 1964.

Hayes, Carlton J. H.   *Essays on Nationalism*. New York: Russell & Russell, 1966. Originally published in 1926.

———.   *The Historical Evolution of Modern Nationalism*. New York: Russell & Russell, 1969. Originally published in 1931.

Hertz, Friedrich O.   *Nationality in History and Politics, A Study of the Psychology and Sociology of National Sentiment and Character*. Oxford, Eng.: Clarendon Press, 1944.

Hinsley, F. H.   *Nationalism and the International System*. London: Hodder & Stoughton, 1973.

Hodges, Donald C., and Shanab, Robert Elias Abu, eds.   *NLF; Na-*

tional Liberation Fronts, 1960/1970. New York: William Morrow & Co., 1972.

Janowsky, Oscar. *Nationalities and National Minorities.* New York: Columbia University Press, 1945.

Kamenka, Eugene, ed. *Nationalism: The Nature and Evolution of an Idea.* Canberra: Australian National University Press, 1973.

Kedourie, Elie. *Nationalism.* Rev. ed. London: Hutchinson University Library, 1961.

Kohn, Hans. *The Idea of Nationalism, A Study in Its Origins and Background.* New York: Collier Books, 1967. Originally published in 1944.

———. *Nationalism, Its Meaning and History.* Rev. ed. Princeton, N.J.: D. Van Nostrand, 1965.

———. *The Age of Nationalism: The First Era of Global History.* New York: Harper & Bros., 1962.

———. *Prophets and Peoples: Studies in Nineteenth Century Nationalism.* New York: Macmillan, 1946.

Minogue, K. R. *Nationalism.* New York: Basic Books, 1967.

Muir, Ramsay. *Nationalism and Internationalism.* London: Constable & Co., 1916.

Rejai, Mostafa, and Enloe, Cynthia H. "Nation-State and State-Nations," *International Studies Quarterly,* vol. 13 (June 1969), pp. 140–58.

Royal Institute of International Affairs. *Nationalism.* Oxford, Eng.: Oxford University Press, 1939.

Shafer, Boyd C. *Nationalism, Myth and Reality.* New York: Harcourt Brace Jovanovich, 1955.

Smith, Anthony D. *Theories of Nationalism.* London: Duckworth, 1971.

Snyder, Louis L. *The Meaning of Nationalism.* New Brunswick, N.J.: Rutgers University Press, 1954.

———, ed. *Dynamics of Nationalism: Readings in Its Meaning and Development.* New York: Van Nostrand Reinhold, 1955.

———. *New Nationalism.* Ithaca, N.Y.: Cornell University Press, 1968.

Sulzbach, Walter. *National Consciousness.* Washington, D.C.: American Council on Public Affairs, 1943.

Tagore, Sir Rabindranath. *Nationalism.* New York: Macmillan Co., 1917.

Ward, Barbara. *Nationalism and Ideology.* New York: W. W. Norton & Co., 1966.

Zangwill, Israel. *The Principle of Nationalities.* London: Watts, 1917.

Znaniecki, Florian. *Modern Nationalities.* Urbana, Ill.: University of Illinois Press, 1952.

3

Democracy

Democracy has evolved over many centuries through modifications both in certain theories that are called democratic and in the practices of a number of countries that are called democratic. And since there are considerable differences among the theories and countries labeled democratic, there are a variety of different meanings of the word *democratic,* depending at least in part upon the political persuasion of the speaker. Some reject the word as referring more accurately to only one type of democracy, direct democracy. These people usually want to replace the word *democratic* with the word *republicanism* or some such word, which they feel refers more accurately to a system of government by elected representatives than does the word *democracy.* Others prefer to see the term *democracy* modified by some other word such as *participatory* to illustrate the need for more activism on the part of the citizenry. Keeping this type of problem in mind, here I shall merely attempt to bring some coherence to this mass of data and opinion. The reader should be aware that neither the approach used nor certain of the conclusions will be acceptable to all, and that other approaches and perhaps other conclusions could have equal, although hopefully not more, validity.

THE PRINCIPLES OF DEMOCRACY

The approach used in the following pages attempts to build a simple model of the key elements of democracy or at least of those elements normally considered significant. They are:

1. Citizen involvement in political decision making.
2. Some degree of equality among citizens.
3. Some degree of liberty or freedom granted to or retained by the citizenry.
4. A system of representation.
5. An electoral system—majority rule.

Citizen involvement

The most fundamental characteristic of any democratic system, truly its defining characteristic, is the idea that the citizens should be involved in some way in the making of political decisions—either directly or through representatives of their choosing. There are two primary considerations—the definition of *citizens* and the degree and means of involvement or participation. The first problem, the definition of citizen, will be discussed with political equality because it is most relevant there. The second problem will be discussed at a number of points. Here let us simply look at the distinctions involved.

1.   *Direct democracy.*   Citizens take part in the actual deliberations and voting on issues, as if the entire population of a country were to debate and pass upon all laws.

2.   *Representative democracy.*   Citizens choose other citizens to debate and pass upon laws.

Citizen involvement can, of course, have a number of dimensions in addition to that described here, such as active participation in a political party or political interest group, or attendance at and participation in public hearings and other political meetings. Even the simple act of discussing politics is an act of involvement in the political process, as is writing to a public official. But as a defining characteristic of democracy, citizen involvement has come to mean either direct or indirect (through the vote) participation in the law-making process.

It must be stressed that citizen involvement is not necessarily limited to the law-making or legislative process. For example, in representative democracy at least part of the executive, such as the President in the United States, is elected and in some countries, particularly in the United States, some judges are elected. Thus, in some approaches to representative democracy, the representative includes members of the executive and judiciary in addition to legislators.

In direct democracy the same thing holds true. Citizens meet together to act as judges in the same way that they meet together to consider laws. And either a separate executive is not considered to be necessary or it is changed at regular and frequent intervals by some such system as choice by lot that keeps it from developing independent power.

The usual criticism of direct democracy and the usual reason given for the development of representative democracy is size. In a large country, geographically or in population, it is simply impossible for the people to meet together.

The basic assumption behind citizen involvement is obviously that a person should be able to have some say about public policy, about things that are done in the name of the public. Also, citizen involvement should ensure that public officials are responsive to changing needs and demands among the citizenry. It does not of course *ensure* that responsiveness, but public officials are likely to be more responsive than they would be otherwise. Finally, involvement is expected to be good for the citizen. If citizens are involved in some way in making decisions, their horizons may broaden; they may gain a feeling of social responsibility; they may become more well-rounded, responsible individuals. It is, of course, unlikely that the simple act of voting will do these things for many people; as a result two other approaches to citizen involvement have developed, elitist theories and participatory theories. The latter, which will be developed later, assert that a much greater degree of involvement is necessary to bring about these advantages—we must recreate direct democracy. The elitist approach, on the other hand, asserts that democracy is "a method of making decisions which insures efficiency in administration and policy making and yet requires some measure of responsiveness to popular opinions on the part of the ruling elites."[1] In this view, citizen involvement is primarily a check on the actions of the political leadership, although there is the possibility for competition for the vote between competing elites. The classical democratic response is that the effects on human beings are of first importance, not efficiency.[2]

Closely related to the elitist approach is pluralism which sees society as composed of groups competing for political power. This competition among groups, and it is sometimes called a system of competing elites, is seen, in pluralism, as the major means of protecting citizen involvement and the rights of the people. The position is that as long as competition exists, and if reasonably fair, no single group or elite can dominate. The current rulers are always kept from taking too much power by the groups or elites who want to replace them. Also, in the making of policy, it is argued that diverse groups with diverse interests keep any one group from too much control. Advocates of pluralism argue that it is a major protection for freedom.

Critics of pluralism make two major points. First, that pluralism represents a cynical disregard of all values except those related to the manipulation of power, and second, that in fact groups cooperate with each other to maintain the present system and are thus obstacles to change.[3]

Equality

Although the issue of equality has been discussed for centuries, it is only within the 20th century that it has taken on cen-

[1] Jack L. Walker, "A Critique of the Elitist Theory of Democracy," *American Political Science Review*, vol. 60 (June 1966), p. 286.

[2] See, for example, Lane Davis, "The Costs of Realism: Contemporary Restatements of Democracy," *Western Political Quarterly*, vol. 17 (March 1964), pp. 37–46. On this issue, see also, Peter Bachrach, *The Theory of Democratic Elitism: A Critique* (Boston: Little, Brown & Co., 1967); Dennis F. Thompson, *The Democratic Citizen; Social Science and Democratic Theory in the Twentieth Century* (New York: Cambridge University Press, 1970); and Carole Pateman, *Participation and Democratic Theory* (New York: Cambridge University Press, 1970).

[3] On the controversy, see David Nicholls, *Three Varieties of Pluralism* (New York: St. Martin's Press, 1974); Henry S. Kariel, *The Decline of American Pluralism* (Stanford: Stanford University Press, 1961); and Marvin E. Olsen, "Social Pluralism as a Basis for Democracy," in Marvin E. Olsen (ed.) *Power in Societies* (New York: Macmillan Co., 1970), pp. 182–88.

tral importance in political theory and practice. It is easy to see that countries, both democratic and nondemocratic all over the world are attempting to achieve a greater degree of equality, or at least the appearance of such equality. But equality is a deceptive idea. It appears simple at first glance, but it is in fact quite complicated. The notion of equality contains five separate ideas that are used in varying combinations—political equality, equality before the law, equality of opportunity, economic equality, and social equality. Not all of these ideas are generally thought of in the strict sense of equality, which is sameness in relevant aspects. This definition is, of course, quite complex because of the phrase "in relevant aspects."[4]

Assuming for the moment the existence of some sort of representative system, we can look at the first and simplest part of equality—political equality—and even this is not very simple. This includes two separate points—equality at the ballot box and equality in the ability to be elected to public office. Equality at the ballot box entails the following:

1. Each individual must have reasonably easy access to the place of voting.
2. All persons must be free to cast their vote as they wish.
3. Each vote must be given exactly the same weight when being counted.

These conditions are rarely fulfilled. First, there is the problem of citizenship that we noted earlier. All those who are not citizens and all those below a certain age are not politically equal. In addition, there are other groups that are formally discriminated against such as certain convicted criminals. At times there have been other legal qualifications for voting added such as owning a specified amount of property. Until relatively recently women also have not been allowed to vote in most democracies and are still not allowed to vote in some.

Finally, there are many informal avenues of inequality. First, and perhaps most obvious, is racial and sexual discrimination. Second, economic inequality acts to limit the poorer voter by limiting his or her ability to participate in the selection of can-

---

[4] See the discussion in J. Roland Pennock and John W. Chapman, eds., *Nomos IX: Equality* (New York: Atherton Press, 1967), particularly the article "Egalitarianism and the Idea of Equality," by Hugo Adam Bedau.

didates. The wealthier voter can significantly affect the campaign effectiveness of a candidate by supporting the campaign financially. Other limitations on the ability of the voter to express his or her desires are less obvious—the difficulty of getting to a polling place affects many older voters, and lack of access to complete information denies many voters the chance to vote for someone who in fact represents their point of view. One issue that has caused considerable debate in the United States over the past few years because it is seen as a possible limitation on the weighting of votes has been reapportionment or the attempt to achieve greater equality in the number of people that each representative represents. For example, it can be argued, to take an extreme case, that a voter in a district with only 100,000 other voters has more chance of affecting the outcome than a voter in a district with 1,000,000 other voters. Thus courts have directed states to attempt to achieve greater equality among legislative districts.

Equality in the ability to be elected to public office normally means that everyone who has the vote is also capable of being elected to public office, although there are usually higher age qualifications and other specific requirements, such as residing in a specified area, for particular offices. In many countries today, it is also becoming very expensive to run for public office, and hence equality in the ability to be elected to public office is being seriously eroded. In most countries, notably in the United States, there have been attempts to limit the effect of wealth on the ability to be elected to public office by legally controlling campaign spending.

Equality before the law resembles the definition of equality as sameness in relevant aspects because it means that all people will be treated in the same way by the legal system, and it is not hedged about by so many formal definitions of relevant aspects. In practice, though, all legal systems have developed a set of informal relevant aspects that depend on such things as wealth, race, or the type of crime involved.

It must be emphasized, though, that a major function of law and legal procedures is to establish general rules that all people are expected to accept and obey or face the consequences. Thus law, by its very nature, is an equalizing force in society if it is enforced fairly.

The third type of equality is related to the social stratification and mobility systems. Equality of opportunity means, first,
that every individual in society will be able to move up or down
within the class or status system depending on ability and the
application of that ability. Second, it means that no *artificial* barrier will keep any person from achieving what ability and hard
work can gain him or her. The connection between these two
is significant because, if equality of opportunity is denied, an
individual will also be denied the ability to move up or down
within the class or status system. The key problem in the definition of equality of opportunity is the word *artificial,* and it has
caused much controversy. Normally *artificial* has been applied
to such characteristics of an individual as race or religion that
do not affect inherent abilities.

Equality of opportunity is a peculiarly complex concept because it is tied to the social stratification and mobility systems
and therefore will vary greatly from society to society. We tend
to think of social status and mobility as fairly easy to measure
because we almost always link them to an easily quantifiable
object—money. In most Western societies today that measure
is a fairly accurate guide to status (except at the level of the
traditional aristocracy) and the major means of gaining or losing status. But even in the West it is not quite so simple. For
example, college professors have traditionally been poorly paid
(and still are) but have had a status somewhat higher than their
income would dictate. In a society according status on the basis
of some other value, such as education, money would not automatically bring status. We must remember that equality of opportunity depends on the value that is accorded status and is
therefore a much more complex notion than it appears at first.

The fourth aspect of equality, economic equality, is very
bothersome. Very few political philosophers have advocated
sameness in this regard, but a thorough discussion of this question cannot ignore this exact definition of economic equality.
Strictly speaking, economic equality could mean that every individual within the society should have the same income. This
definition is normally avoided because most advocates of economic equality are more concerned with the political and legal
aspects of equality and equality of opportunity than with economic equality. In addition, complete equality of income would

be unfair to all individuals because it would not take into account that different individuals have different needs. If the income level were sufficiently high, these differences in need might be irrelevant because everyone would have enough no matter what his or her needs might be, but this is the only way in which the problem of differential need could be overcome.

The usual argument for economic equality is that every individual within a society must be guaranteed a minimum level of economic security because without security, liberty and the other equalities that are essential to democracy are impossible. The stress here is on security, not equality, and the degree of security varies tremendously.

The major contention, the key to the whole argument for economic equality in this sense, is the contention that without some degree of economic security the democratic system cannot operate in a democratic manner. Clearly, economic inequality does have an effect on the operation of the democratic system. The question is whether the effect is great enough to change the system from democracy to something else. Most people today will argue that a too great inequality of income will do this. How great an inequality is permissible and by what means do you bring the extremes closer together are the crucial issues. We shall look at these problems in greater detail as we discuss the differences between democratic capitalism and democratic socialism.

Extreme levels of poverty effectively bar an individual from participation in the life of the community. This is peculiarly significant in education. It has been found that a child in a typical middle-class or lower middle-class home has had toys and other objects that help to teach many of the skills that are essential to learn easily. A simple thing such as having a book read aloud a number of times shows the child the turning of the pages of the book and normally will indicate that the English language is read from left to right and will thus tend to set up a pattern which his or her eyes will follow.

The child who has not had any of this will start out a year or two or even three behind the more fortunate child. There are also certain skills that a child learns in playing with toys that are essential even for relatively unskilled jobs. A child fitting together pieces of a puzzle or parts of a toy is learning skills that the other child will have to struggle to learn later. It has been found that a child from the poverty areas may not even have seen a mirror and may thus have no self-identity, having no idea what he or she, as an individual, looks like. The effect of this on a child's life can be profound, and we are un- sure as to whether some of these effects can be reversed for the child who is already in our school systems. Thus, children at five or six may already have handicaps that they will never be able to lose. They may already have lost the possibility to develop their full potentials. There are exceptions. There are children who are brought up after generations in this sort of poverty who do make it. However, the overwhelming majority do not make it and in all probability cannot make it because they have simply lost out to the children of parents who can afford simple toys and books and the time to spend with their children.

The fifth type of equality, social equality, is in some ways the most difficult to define because no one seems to be quite clear about what it means. In a narrow sense, perhaps, it can be said that social equality means that no public or private association may erect artificial barriers to activity within the association. Again, there is the problem of defining *artificial,* but generally we use it in about the same sense as above, that is, denoting characteristics, such as race or religion, that do not affect an individual's inherent abilities. Examples of this type of equality might be the lack of artificial barriers to membership in a coun- try club or in the use of a public park. Social equality refers to the absence of the class and status distinctions that have been and still are recognized throughout every society. In this sense it includes aspects of equality of opportunity.

As such, it is a fairly intangible thing. It means that a wide variety of people with different backgrounds, positions, and in- comes can get together and all be accepted. Again, we raise the problem of what are artificial and what might be meaning- ful barriers to this type of equality. Poverty may become a meaningful barrier even though it might have started as an artificial one. A poverty-stricken individual and an individual from the middle class or lower middle class would have a very difficult time associating with each other because they come from radically different cultures. But this is really an artificial barrier. Complete social equality would mean that the gap could be bridged, that the cultural differences could be overcome and made unimportant or accepted as valuable differences.

Liberty

Historically, the desire for equality has often been expressed as an aspect of liberty. When Thomas Jefferson, drafting the Declaration of Independence, spoke of equality, he meant that people were equal in the rights they had. Equality of opportunity is often thought of as a right. On the other hand, many people believe that attempts to achieve a degree of economic equality are directly in conflict with attempts to maintain economic liberty, and this problem will be discussed in more detail in the sections on democratic capitalism and democratic socialism. But the important point here is the perceived conflict between aspects of equality and aspects of liberty. Thus, there are many ways in which liberty and equality are closely connected in democratic theory. But, in order to understand more fully the ramifications of this curious interrelationship, we are going to examine the idea of liberty much more closely.

Liberty, freedom, and *right* are often used interchangeably. Although some scholars prefer to make a careful distinction among the meanings of the three words, it is not necessary to do so. All three terms refer to the ability to act without restriction or with restriction that is itself limited in specified or at least specifiable ways. *Freedom* is the most general term and refers to all aspects of unfettered action. *Liberty* usually is used to refer to social and political freedom. *Right* usually refers to specific legally guaranteed freedoms.

There probably is no such thing as complete freedom. In the first place, one must maintain life and perform a number of essential bodily functions. Within limits it is possible to choose the times at which one eats, drinks, sleeps, and so on, but one cannot ignore them altogether. In the second place, there are other people. Although they are essential for a complete life, they do restrict one. There is an old adage that "Your freedom to swing your arm stops at my nose." Although it is superficial, it does point out that the existence of others must be taken into account and that they do restrict one.

Probably the most influential approach to liberty can be found in the distinctions between the rights that a human being has or should have and the rights derived from government. The former are often called natural rights; the latter are called civil rights. Although the trend today is either to reject the concept of natural rights altogether and call all rights civil rights or to replace the word *natural* with *human,* it is still instructive to look at the traditional distinction.

Many democratic theorists, such as John Locke,[5] argued that human beings as human beings, separate from all government or society, had certain rights which should never be given up or taken away.[6] People, they argued, could never give up these rights upon joining a society or government, and the society or government should not attempt to take these rights away. If a government did try to take them away, the people were perfectly justified in revolting to change the government, although not all argued for this last point. The most important point is that natural rights establish limits. The Bill of Rights in the United States Constitution is a good example of this point. In many cases the amendment in the Bill of Rights says "Congress shall make no law regarding . . . ." The wording clearly indicates a limit on governmental activity at a fundamental level. A recent scholar, Isaiah Berlin, has called this approach "negative liberty." By this he meant the area of life within which one "is or should be left to do or be what he is able to do or be, without interference by other persons."[7] Here I have stressed the tradition in the United States that emphasizes possible interference from government. Thus certain areas of life, such as speech, religion, press, and assembly, have been clearly defined as areas of "negative liberty" where one is left alone to do, on the whole, what one wants.

Berlin also develops a concept that he calls "positive liberty." As used by Berlin this concept refers to the possibility of indi-

---

[5] John Locke (1632–1704), author of *Two Treatises of Civil Government,* which was widely acclaimed by the authors of the American Constitution.

[6] Here I have used the form of argument employed by the so-called social contract theorists because they had a great influence on the development of the notion of liberty in Western thought. See J. W. Gough, *The Social Contract; A Critical Study of Its Development.* 2d ed. (Oxford, Eng.: Clarendon Press, 1957).

[7] Isaiah Berlin, "Two Concepts of Liberty," in his *Four Essays on Liberty* (London: Oxford University Press, 1969), pp. 121–22.

viduals controlling their own destiny, to their ability to choose this or that option. For Berlin this is primarily the area of rational self-control or "self-mastery," as he puts it. For others, this has meant providing conditions for individuals to develop themselves. "Positive liberty" has meant governmental activity to provide the conditions for the full development of the individual.[8]

This approach has also developed from the natural rights tradition, particularly the idea of the right to life. The right to life can be interpreted to mean that every person has a right to the necessary minimum of food, clothing, and shelter that is required to live in a given society. Since standards vary considerably from society to society, the necessary minimum might vary a great deal. From this perspective the right to life might include the right to an education equal to one's ability and the right to a job. Normally, the right to life is not developed this fully, but these examples illustrate the complexity of such generalizations. Other natural rights, such as those to happiness or property, also have been widely debated but have remained unclarified.

Although there was widespread disagreement on the specific natural rights, it was generally agreed that after the formation of government, these rights must become civil rights or rights that were specifically guaranteed and protected by the government even, or particularly, against itself. This formulation of liberty obviously raises many problems. Probably the most basic difficulty is found in the assumption that a government will be willing to guarantee rights against itself, but many thinkers have assumed that representative democracy with fairly frequent elections would solve the problem. Any such government would theoretically recognize that an infringement on people's civil rights would ensure its defeat in the next election. Experience has shown that this is not necessarily true, and the result has been apathy, civil disobedience,[9] and revolu-

---

[8] See, for example, the argument in Christian Bay, *The Structure of Freedom* (Stanford: Stanford University Press, 1958).

[9] See, for example, Mohandas K. Gandhi, *Non-Violent Resistance (Satyagraha)* (New York: Schocken Books, 1951); Joan V. Bondurant, *Conquest of Violence. The Gandhian Philosophy of Conflict,* rev. ed., (Berkeley: University of California Press, 1965; Michael P. Smith and Kenneth L. Deutsch, eds., *Political Obligation and Civil Disobedience: Readings* (New York: Thomas Y.

tion.[10] At the same time, the protection of liberties is still considered to be one of the primary duties of a democratic political system and a central part of democratic theory.

It is somewhat more difficult to define types of liberty than it was to discuss types of equality but, loosely, civil rights seem to include the following specific liberties or freedoms:

Right to vote.

Freedom of speech.

Freedom of the press.

Freedom of religion.

Freedom of movement.

Freedom of assembly.

Freedom from abritrary treatment by the political and legal system.

The first six of these are clearly areas of life which the democratic argument says should be left to the discretion of the individual. Freedom of speech, press, religion, and assembly are very commonly spelled out as areas of individual decision making. Freedom of movement is less commonly included, but may be as important since the ability to move freely about a country is undoubtedly a major protection for other freedoms. The right to vote without interference is, of course, the key to the ability to change the system.

The last freedom, freedom from arbitrary treatment by the political and legal system, is also a major protection for the other freedoms. All democratic societies have clearly estab-

---

Crowell, 1972); the various works of Martin Luther King, Jr., such as *Strength to Love* (New York: Harper & Row, 1963, 1958), *Stride Toward Freedom* (New York: Harper & Row, 1953), *Where Do We Go from Here?* (New York: Harper & Row, 1967), and *Why We Can't Wait* (New York: Harper & Row, 1963); and Elliot M. Zashin, *Civil Disobedience and Democracy* (New York: Free Press, 1972).

[10] See, for example, John Dunn, *Modern Revolutions, An Introduction to the Analysis of a Political Phenomenon* (Cambridge, Eng.: Cambridge University Press, 1972). The bibliography on pp. 295–335 in this book is the best list of the literature available. See also, Mostafa Rejai, *The Strategy of Political Revolution* (Garden City, N.Y.: Doubleday & Co., 1973); Peter Calvert, *Revolution* (London: Macmillan & Co., 1970); Jack Woddis, *New Theories of Revolution; A Commentary on the Views of Frantz Fanon, Regis Debray, and Herbert Marcuse* (New York: International Publishers, 1972); Mark N. Hagopian, *The Phenomenon of Revolution* (New York: Dodd, Mead & Co., 1974)

lished *procedural* rights that are designed to guarantee that every individual will be treated fairly by the system. Without these procedural rights the *substantive* rights of freedom of speech, press, and so on would likely be meaningless.

Most recently, the development of the notion of freedom within the United States has been in the context of legally defined and enforceable rights. Many court decisions, often highly controversial, have gradually changed—sometimes expanded, sometimes reduced—the areas in which an individual citizen or group can expect the legal system to be concerned with their rights.

Another important aspect of liberty is that there is no peculiarly democratic social organization except in the very loose sense that a democratic society should be fairly free and open rather than controlled. It is the general assumption of democratic theory that whatever does no damage to the society as a whole or to the individuals within it should be the concern of no one but the individual or individuals involved.

This means that there is no peculiarly democratic family organization. It further means a broad tolerance for varying belief systems. This tolerance of diverse belief systems tends toward the separation of church and state, to freedom of inquiry within the educational system, and also to the freedom of the mass media to publish or broadcast without censorship. It will be clear to anyone minimally aware of the state of the world today that no democracy actually achieves these ideals.

Finally, the social stratification and social mobility systems must be flexible and open to anyone depending solely on ability and hard work. As we saw in our discussion of equality of opportunity, no democratic system in the world has actually achieved this broad tolerance of diversity within the social system, even if tolerance means simply the acceptance of this diversity, not the approval of it. Therefore, tolerance is merely one stage in a continuum of attitudes toward diversity. Tolerance varies considerably from country to country. Comparative research has shown a wide diversity in such probable indicators of tolerance as freedom of press and speech, and so forth. All these systems, but particularly the social stratification and social mobility systems, are strongly influenced by the peculiarities of the economic systems.

Two other areas of freedom should be noted briefly, the silence of the law and the problem of unenforceability. It is part of the Anglo-American tradition that unless there is a law prohibiting an action, that action is within the area of individual discretion until such a law is written. And when the law is written it cannot affect actions that came prior to it. Also, the experience of prohibition in the United States indicated that there are unenforceable laws, laws that people simply won't accept. This also should be seen as an aspect of freedom.

Each of these liberties is limited to some extent by all political systems. The democratic system has built into it certain safeguards that are supposed to protect individuals from having their freedoms too severely restricted. Of course they do not always work. The most fundamental of these safeguards is the basic characteristic of a democracy—the people have some control over their government. Democratic theorists have never adequately dealt with the problem of severe restrictions of rights when they are desired by or acquiesced in by the majority. In modern representative democracies, this problem is made more complex because of the various roles assumed by the representatives. Therefore, we will look at the representative system next.

The system of representation

The most obvious problem with direct democracy was that it appeared to be able only to function in a country that was fairly small, both in territory and population.[11] Because of this difficulty, a number of theories developed suggesting that this problem could be overcome by one individual representing an area or a number of people. Since this approach seemed to be a practical solution to the problem it was widely adopted, and therefore contemporary democracy is sometimes called representative democracy. Theories of representation[12] are virtually as complex as democracy itself. There are three senses in which

---

[11] For a recent study of this question, see Robert A. Dahl and Edward R. Tufte, *Size and Democracy* (Stanford, Calif.: Stanford University Press, 1973).

[12] See Hanna Fenichal Pitkin, *The Concept of Representation* (Berkeley, Calif.: University of California Press, 1967) and A. H. Birch, *Representation* (New York: Praeger, 1971).

the word *represent* is used that help provide an understanding of the problem. First, we often say that something represents something else when it is a faithful reproduction or an exact copy of the original. Second, we use the word *represent* in the sense of an object symbolizing another object. Third, we sometimes use the word *represent* in the sense of a lawyer acting for or in place of his client. These three senses of representation, particularly the differences between the first and the third, reveal much of the problem that representation holds for democratic theory. In addition, the following selection, taken from a famous speech of Edmund Burke to the Electors of Bristol, illustrates a further distinction that bothers theorists of representation and practical politicians alike:

> To deliver an opinion is the right of all men; that of constituents is a weighty and respectable opinion, which a representative ought always rejoice to hear, and which he ought always most seriously to consider. But *authoritative* instructions, *mandates* issued, which the member is bound blindly and implicitly to obey, to vote, and to argue for, though contrary to the dearest conviction of his judgment and conscience—these are things utterly unknown to the laws of this land, and which arise from a fundamental mistake of the whole order and tenor of our Constitution.
>
> Parliament is not a *congress* of ambassadors from different and hostile interests, which each must maintain, as an agent and advocate, against other agents and advocates; but Parliament is a *deliberative* assembly of *one* nation, with one interest, that of the whole where not local purposes, not local prejudices, ought to guide, but the general good, resulting from the general reason of the whole. You choose a member, indeed; but when you have chosen him, he is not a member of Bristol, but he is a member of *Parliament*. If the local constituent should form a hasty opinion evidently opposite to the real good of the rest of the community, the member for that place ought to be as far as any other from an endeavor to give it effect.[13]

Here Burke presents a case for the representative as an independent agent who represents something solely in the sense that he or she is elected by the people in a particular area. In doing this, he specifically rejects representation in the sense

---

[13] Speech to the Electors of Bristol (1774) in *The Works of the Right Honorable Edmund Burke,* 7th ed. (Boston: Little, Brown & Co., 1881), vol. II, p. 96. Emphasis in the original.

of our third definition of agent for some individual or group. A fifth theory might be added, composed of elements of all but Burke's position. It is sometimes argued that the representative should be a microcosm of the multiplicity of interests that are found in his constituency, with each interest being part of him to the exact extent that it is important within his district. As unlikely as this is, some representatives try to achieve it. Seldom, if ever, will it be true that an elected official will fit exactly one, and only one, of the roles assigned by these theories of representation. Even the most Burkean of representatives will act as an agent for his constituency at times or on certain issues if he expects to be reelected.[14] The typical representative is likely to act as an agent for his constituents whenever they are actively concerned with a particular issue with which he has to deal. He is also likely to act as an agent in assisting individuals or groups of his constituents when they are dealing with the bureaucracy and need assistance. At the same time, the typical representative is likely to act as the Burkean representative on issues that do not directly concern his constituency (thus on which he receives little or no pressure from his constituency) and to act in what he believes to be the best interest of the nation as a whole.

Thus, these five differing definitions of representation, all of which have played and still do play important roles in the various theories and systems of representation, influence the structure and operation of democratic government.

One of the key issues within representative democracy is the concern of some theorists to equate representative and direct democracy. In the U.S. system such practices as the initiative, referendum, and recall[15] were developed as devices to

---

[14] See David H. Davidson, The Role of the Congressman (New York: Pegasus, 1969), pp. 110–42; Donald R. Matthews, U.S. Senators and Their World (New York: Vintage Books, 1960), pp. 218–42; and Charles L. Clapp, The Congressman; His Work as He Sees It (Washington, D.C.: Brookings Institution, 1963), pp. 50–103.

[15] Initiative—a method by which a new law may be proposed directly by the voters by means of a petition. Referendum—a method by which the voters may pass on legislation already passed by a legislative body. Recall—a method by which an official may be removed from office during his term by a vote of the people. Impeachment, or the likelihood thereof, is, of course, another means by which an official can be removed from office during his term.

allow the people as a whole to play a direct role in political decision making. This problem can perhaps be seen most clearly in the thinking of Jean Jacques Rousseau. At one point he says, "Thus deputies of the people are not, and cannot be, its representatives; they are merely its agents, and can make no final decisions. Any law which the people have not ratified in person is null, it is not a law."[16] Here Rousseau has used two of our definitions of *represent*. For him *represent* cannot refer to an agent but must refer to one who acts only with constituent approval. But Rousseau realized that within a large country direct democracy was impractical, even impossible, and, although he maintains the ideal of direct democracy, he does discuss representation in a more favorable light. He says:

> I have just shown that government weakens as the number of magistrates [read elected officials] increases; and I have already shown that the more numerous the people is, the more repressive force is needed. From which it follows that the ratio of magistrates to government should be in inverse proportion to the ratio of subjects to sovereign; which means that the more the state expands, the more the government ought to contract; and thus that the number of rulers should diminish in proportion to the increases of the population.[17]

If possible Rousseau would like to see a country small enough so that every man could be his own representative, but as population rises this becomes more and more difficult. Thus the number of rulers must of necessity diminish through the establishment of some type of representative system. But he strongly believes that the closer a system can come to a direct democracy through an increase in the number of magistrates, the better the system will be.[18]

Rousseau's approach to representation has regained favor in recent years in the movement known as participatory democracy. This movement has emphasized both the benefits that

---

[16] Jean Jacques Rousseau, *De Contrat social* (Paris: La Renaissance de Livre [1762]), p. 86. Rousseau (1712–78) was a famous French political philosopher best known for his work *De Contrat social (The Social Contract)*.

[17] Ibid., p. 59.

[18] See Rousseau's discussion of such a system in *Projet de constitution pour la Corse* ("Constitutional Project for Corsica"), in Jean Jacques Rousseau, *Political Writings*, trans. and ed. Frederick Watkins (London: Thomas Nelson & Sons, 1953), pp. 277–330.

accrue to the individual from actively participating in the political life of the community and the need, following Rousseau, to break up our political units into smaller segments that will be able to deal more directly with the problems that people must face in their immediate environment. This should, it is argued, force the political system to be more responsive to the needs of the people. The initiative, referendum, and recall were earlier attempts to bring about the same result. The participatory democrat argues that individuals should not be bound by laws that they did not help to make or participate in making. In other words, the individual, all individuals, must be consulted in the making of laws that will affect them. If they are not consulted, the law is considered invalid. The law is also considered invalid if the individual feels that it is unjust. This is again an attempt to make the representative more responsive to the wishes of constituents and, in a broader sense, to bring the whole representative system more in line with the ideals of direct democracy.[19]

Electoral system

In a discussion of representation, it is important to emphasize the primary purpose of the representative system in a democracy; that is, to provide a means for citizens to exercise some control over political decision making when they cannot directly exercise it themselves. This means, since the representative will not automatically be expected to serve for life, some method must be devised so that the people can either maintain the representative in, or remove him or her from, office. This brings us to the institution of periodic elections. Many scholars argue that the electoral system is a major defining characteristic of a democracy,[20] particularly the system by which the majority rules. The electoral system is as important an issue in democratic theory as the theory of representation because it is the primary way of ensuring some governmental responsiveness to the wishes of the people. In a large, complex

---

[19] For references on participatory democracy, see the Suggested Readings at the end of Chapter 7.

[20] For example, see Henry B. Mayo, *An Introduction to Democratic Theory* (New York: Oxford University Press, 1960), pp. 72–106.

society, the vote may be the only way in which the majority of the people ever participate in political decision making.

With a few exceptions the specific institutional arrangements of elections are not of much importance, but the exceptions are noteworthy. The normal rule of elections is clearly that the side with the most votes wins, but this seemingly clear principle of majority rule is in fact fairly complicated. First, it in no way assumes that the 50% + 1 of the voters is right and the 50% − 1 is wrong. It merely says that since more people voted for A rather than B, A must be temporarily accepted.

Unfortunately, this point is not always recognized; furthermore, it tends to assume that any issue has only two sides. If, for example, there are three candidates in any given election, majority rule becomes more complicated since it is harder to clearly determine what the majority wants. Since relatively few potential voters actually cast their ballot in many elections, the majority may not actually be represented in the result. This objection may, of course, be answered that those who do not vote, do not care, but it might also be answered that their desires were not represented by any side in the election. This difficulty indicates the advantage of having more than two candidates in an election, but we have already seen the disadvantage of such an arrangement—if no one receives a clear majority, does this constitute majority rule? Thus, at times various governments have made it difficult or even impossible for more than two sides to be represented on the ballot. An additional institutional arrangement that raises serious questions since it allows minority veto, is the common practice in the United States of requiring more than a simple majority on certain issues, particularly on money issues. This is, of course, almost always the case in amending basic sets of rules, such as constitutions. The major purpose behind this is to protect the rights of the minority, it being felt that a minority with strongly held opinions should not be dictated to by the majority.

Again, this raises the whole problem of participation in the political system. The electoral system, although seemingly only a mechanism for determining the composition of the government over the next few years, actually provides the major and sometimes the sole means of political participation for individuals living within a large, complex, modern society such as the

United States. Hence the electoral system takes on peculiar importance for democratic theory because, if it does provide a significant or even the only means of political participation for an individual, it is the key to whether the system is democratic or not. An individual, when entering the voting booth, must be sure that his or her vote will be counted, that he or she is voting in an election that provides some choice, and that the choice is meaningful in the sense that the voter is actually free to vote for any of the options that are provided. It is also important to remember the most obvious point; that is, the individual is allowed to vote in the first place.

Finally, each individual's vote should be equal to any other individual's vote. This is disputed by some who, believing themselves to be democratic, argue that since there are individuals who are worth more to the community than the normal run-of-the-mill citizen, these individuals should be provided with more votes on the basis of some formula such as the amount of taxes paid.[21] This argument is not a common one by any means, but it illustrates the important point that there are fundamental disagreements over all aspects of the electoral system. Not everyone is allowed to vote within any country. There are commonly elections in every country in which there is only one candidate, and as we have seen there are those who contend that not all votes should be counted equally.

These questions of electoral procedure imply other important problems. The electoral system, in addition to providing a means of political participation, is significant because it guarantees the means for the peaceful change of political power from one individual or group to another. This in turn raises the whole problem of leadership within a democracy, a question confronting democratic theorists since ancient Athens. The importance of leadership in democratic theory cannot be gainsaid, and in representative democracy it is peculiarly significant. Whatever theory of representation is accepted, the elected official is given some political power that is not directly held by constituents. This power can be removed through the electoral process but, in the meantime, it is held by an individual who

---

[21] Mark Twain once wrote a short satirical sketch on this point. See "The Curious Republic of Gondour," *Atlantic Monthly*, vol. 36 (October 1875), pp. 461–63. Recently reprinted in Arthur O. Lewis, ed., *American Utopias: Selected Short Fiction* (New York: Arno Press and *The New York Times*, 1971).

can thus directly participate in political decision making to the extent of the power invested in his or her office. In addition, this officer may also exercise political leadership in the sense that he or she can help to form or inform the opinions of constituents and others by defining the political issues that he or she believes significant and by propagandizing for particular positions.[22]

Historically, most democratic theorists have been concerned to limit the political power held by any one individual or group within the society while at the same time providing intelligent and capable leadership. For example, James Madison (1751–1836), an important figure in the framing of the U.S. Constitution, was greatly worried about the possibility of some faction, including a "majority faction," gaining political power and exercising it in their own interest. Thus, Madison and most of the other writers of the Constitution advocated an enlightened leadership of aristocracy exercising political power but periodically checked through election, rather than rule by the people. In other words, they accepted Burke's theory of representation and made it the essence of their theory of government.

DEMOCRACY AND NATIONALISM

One of the peculiarities of all contemporary political ideologies is the manner in which they are each affected by nationalism. Democracy is no exception, although it may be said to affect the practice of countries more than the ideology. In the United States, when speaking of the phenomenon known as nationalism, we usually use *patriotism* when we approve of the action and *nationalism* when we disapprove of the action. Such distinctions are, of course, inherently false since closely related phenomena are involved in each case, but the use of *patriotism* as an equivalent to *nationalism* should help the American reader to recognize what we are talking about. Americans are familiar with the sort of oratory that is presented to them on the occasion of Fourth of July speeches. Contemporary readers may not be as familiar with the type of nationalism or patriotism that was common earlier in U.S. history.

---

[22] On the problem of leadership, see Ralph M. Stogdill, *Handbook of Leadership; A Survey of Theory and Research* (New York: Free Press, 1974).

Historians speak of a certain period as the period of "manifest destiny." Many people believed that U.S. citizens were a chosen people specially selected to rule most if not all of the North American continent and whose example could be the salvation of Europe, which many believed to be the center of decadence. Many examples of this can be seen in American history and the history of other democracies, such as that of the United Kingdom. In the United States, we have the example of the desire to save the world for democracy in World War I and at a variety of other times. There is also the current, widespread belief that the United States must act as a world policeman. And, of course, there is the belief that institutions in the United States are somehow better than those of other countries, that Americans are more free, more equal, and, on the whole, more democratic and even better than others.

Americans tend to view democracy as peculiarly American and feel that any nondemocratic institution or any change away from democracy anywhere in the world threatens the American system. There is also an intense nationalism or patriotism attached, at least in some circles, to the American economic system. Many people believe that capitalism or the "mixed economy," as the economic system in the United States is sometimes called, is better, more just, and certainly more efficient than any other economic system. Americans also tend to equate the United States and democracy, often believing that the United States must save the world for democracy, particularly from the threat of communism, even by force if necessary. This is in part due to the belief in the inherent superiority of capitalism as an economic system; since relatively few countries in the world look favorably on capitalism, perhaps U.S. capitalists feel somewhat beleaguered, threatened, and defensive about their system.

DEMOCRACY AND THE ECONOMIC SYSTEM[23]

Probably the most controversial topic among those who consider themselves to be democrats is which economic system

---

[23] For further material on this large topic, see the Suggested Readings at the end of the chapter.

is more democratic—capitalism or socialism. In the next few pages we will look at each contender, not with a view to settling the issue, but simply with an attempt to understand what the debate is all about.

Democracy and capitalism

Capitalism is an economic system that has changed greatly over the years. Traditionally, it meant a system characterized by:

1. Private ownership of property.
2. No limitation on the accumulation of property.
3. The absence of governmental intervention in the economy—the free market system.

Today capitalism is characterized by:

1. Most property held privately.
2. Little actual limit on the accumulation of property.
3. Governmental *regulation* of the economy—a modified free market system.
4. A growing welfare system.

The distinctions between these two systems must be kept in mind because many discussions of capitalism confuse the picture by mixing the two systems. Traditional capitalism does not exist in North America or Europe today, but too many people talk about capitalism as if it were still the traditional system.

Capitalists of both persuasions see the major democratic aspect of capitalism in liberty, but they approach it differently. For example, the defenders of traditional capitalism contend that the whole edifice of liberty is founded upon private property and would be destroyed either if the amount of property that can be held by any one individual were limited or the free market system were interfered with in any way. Since government is the only organization powerful enough to limit property holding, this question logically shifts to the problem of governmental intervention in the economy. The modern capitalist argues along slightly different lines. He or she might argue that a limit on property would infringe liberty and would change the traditional system, but agree that some sort of limit can be put on the amount held by any given individual. This would enable more people to hold property and hence would provide a broader base for liberty. The free market system can be modified by powerful economic entities such as monopolies or large multinational corporations, but the traditional capitalist argues that the danger from government is greater since governmental interference is not responsive to changes in the market while corporations are. Some argue for a role for government in fostering competitive markets.[24]

Modern capitalists also argue that the more widespread property holding is within the system, the more viable capitalism is. The amount of property and money that individuals hold directly affects the amount of money that they spend. The amount of money that they spend directly affects the amount that any industry can produce; the amount that they produce obviously affects the number of people that they can hire; the number of people they can hire again affects the amount of money that is in the system, and thus can be spent for the products of the company; the amount of products that the company can produce obviously then affects the profit of the company. In this way, it is argued that some limitation on the amount of property or money that can be held by any individual can in fact help the entire capitalist system rather than be a detriment to it because it forces the money to circulate more widely.

A second argument centers on governmental intervention in the economy, particularly in the sense of governmental regulation of the economy. The argument of traditional capitalists remains the same. Any governmental intervention in the economy, they contend, would destroy the basis for the capitalist system; hence, individualism and liberty. But the defenders of some governmental regulation (although as opposed to control) of the economy, say that the complete absence of governmental regulation acts itself to destroy the democratic capitalist system because a very few people would be able to control the economy and even the government through the establishment of monopolies. Many other bad effects of a lack of governmental regulation are mentioned, but the development of monopolies is the most important politically.

---

[24] See, for example, Milton Friedman, *Capitalism and Freedom* (Chicago: University of Chicago Press, 1962), p. 2.

The problem of monopolies is illustrated in the United States in the period of the great expansion of the railroads and of industrialism in general. Such men as J. P. Morgan, J. J. Hill, and the Rockefellers virtually controlled the American economy and by doing so the American government. This monopolistic tendency, the modern capitalist would argue, destroys the capitalist system by radically limiting the number of companies or individuals who can adequately compete within the system. It is not a capitalist system when a few companies can set the prices on virtually all the goods within a country because relatively few new men with new ideas or approaches would be able to experiment with them in the system. It would not be talent that would show in the system, it would be the monopolist's will. This does not fit the myth of the capitalist system of the office boy who becomes corporation president through diligent work. The office boy of a monopolist might become a business president someday, but not necessarily by diligent work. The key factor would be the whim of the monopolist, not the talent of the office boy.

Thus, although the monopoly system cannot be seen as the ideal of capitalism, it is the system that totally unregulated capitalism tended to become.[25] Probably the most important effect of monopoly, viewed from the perspective of democratic theory, is the control of the government that could be exercised by the monopolist. Such control would obviously severely restrict the degree to which democracy could exist because it might even negate the effect of popular participation in political decision making. President Eisenhower, in his farewell address, warned the American people about a military-industrial complex that he contended was close to ruling the United States through informal channels. This is the sort of thing that could happen even more readily under a monopoly system.[26] Thus, although regulation of monopolies is not the only form of governmental intervention in the economy, for our purpose it is the most significant.

---

[25] For a different view see Gabriel Kolko, *The Triumph of Conservatism; A Reinterpretation of American History, 1900–1916* (New York: Free Press, 1963).

[26] The New Left contends that it has already happened. See Chapter 7 and Paul A. Baran and Paul M. Sweezy, *Monopoly Capital; An Essay on the American Economic and Social Order* (New York: Monthly Review Press, 1966).

Modern capitalism is often called a mixed economy, which indicates that, although most property is held privately, extensive property may be publicly owned. It also signifies that the government, the public, may be active in the manufacturing and distribution of goods, even though this is also primarily in private hands. The emphasis, though, is on regulation rather than ownership, manufacturing, or distribution. The changes in capitalism from the traditional to the mixed system are all changes in degree, not in kind. Private ownership is still the major means of property holding; wealth is somewhat limited by the system of taxation, but immense fortunes can still be accumulated. Unquestionably, government does intervene extensively in the economy, but it is supposed to act primarily to ensure that the game is played fairly and to see that the losers do not starve.

Of course, there are many who contend that this is not the manner in which the government in the democratic capitalist system, particularly in the United States, does intervene, but that it intervenes for reasons that relate more to control than to regulation.

There are those who also argue that the government does not see that the game is played fairly, but that it supports certain of the players who do not play fairly. In addition, it should be noted that regulation of such an enormous operation as the capitalist system in the United States is virtually impossible. No one can know everything that is going on. No governmental agency, however efficient, can keep its fingers on all the possible questionable dealings. Regulation, then, is of necessity somewhat sporadic, but the modern capitalist would argue that even this sporadic regulation helps to avoid the excesses of monopoly.

Capitalism has changed; there can be no question of that, but it still exists and will exist as long as the private sector of the economy is larger than the public. Whether or not it is a good system is not the question here. We are only concerned with description and with the relationship between capitalism and democracy. The latter can be stated quite simply. Capitalism as an economic system is not *directly* concerned with participation in political decision making. On the other hand, capitalism is directly concerned with equality and liberty. Equality of opportunity is stressed and there is concern with economic freedom in the sense that each person is freely and equally able to enter the marketplace and succeed or fail on the basis of ability and the consumer's desire and need for his or her product or service.

In this light it would seem, at least on the surface, a little foolish to speak of capitalism as a particularly democratic system. Why then do so many people believe that capitalism is the only system that can fit with a democratic political system? There are, of course, many arguments based on patriotic feelings about the democratic capitalist system of the United States. Many argue that because the United States has been economically and politically successful, the combination of systems that exists in this country has to be the best.

This sort of argument is questionable at best, and we must look for sounder reasons. The main argument stems from the belief that capitalism allows more freedom for the individual than does any other economic system. Any individual with sufficient interest and funds can buy stock in any number of companies within a democratic capitalist system, in this way becoming part of the working of the economy. He or she becomes part owner of a company or companies and can, if time and money permit, participate in some decisions of the company at the annual meetings, although this ability is limited for the small shareholder. It is also possible for any individual with the money and the energy to go into business. If the individual has a product that people want, he or she may be successful. If the person has a product that people either do not want or cannot afford, he or she will fail. But the point is not the success or the failure, but that the system allows the individual to make an attempt, even though it may or may not offer encouragement, depending on the circumstances of the times.

In addition, there are those who argue that capitalism provides greater political freedom than any other system. "The kind of economic organization that provides economic freedom directly, namely, competitive capitalism, also promotes political freedom because it separates economic power from political power and in this way enables the one to offset the other."[27] This can be compared to a check and balance system such as that intended in the American Constitution. If both eco-

---

[27] Friedman, *Capitalism and Freedom*, p. 9.

nomic and political power is centralized in government, there is no check on the activities of government except through the vote. In this approach, governmental power is checked by centers of economic power, which check each other, and are in turn checked by government which is also limited by regular elections.

There is the freedom of the individual to enter the economic system, again under some governmental regulation and some limitation due to the existence of many large corporations; to succeed or fail upon his or her own willingness to work hard and the desire of the consumer, manipulated to some extent by advertising, to buy the product. This freedom is overwhelmingly an economic freedom. This is one of the main reasons why capitalism is primarily concerned with equality of opportunity; the system says that every person should be able to become a capitalist and have the potential of getting rich.

Because of this concern with equality of opportunity, the mixed economy has recently begun to develop a welfare system designed to ensure that everyone within the society will actually have an equal opportunity to succeed. This concern is not solely based on humanitarian ends but also on the recognition that people who cannot provide for themselves are in fact a burden on society and a tremendous waste of potential manpower. In addition, welfare programs have been concerned with the aged, who have contributed to society but who need help to provide for their retirement when many costs, such as medical bills, tend to rise and their incomes decline. This welfare system has been developed more thoroughly and less haphazardly under democratic socialism because it has been concerned with a broader definition of equality than has democratic capitalism.

Welfare systems around the world are coming under tremendous criticism recently for doing exactly what they were designed to do, for being *welfare* systems that give away money rather than provide an individual with the means of earning it. This sort of criticism is particularly appropriate and common in the capitalist system because, in effect it is saying that this welfare system is not providing the equality of opportunity that capitalism desires. What it is actually doing is removing people from the mainstream of economic life, giving them a subsistence on which to live and not allowing them to enter the capitalist system even at the most minimal level of wage earner.

Today the system is also being criticized on different grounds by the recipients of the welfare. They have recognized how it keeps them in a state of poverty, not allowing them to get out. The recipients of the welfare system have also been treated poorly by the bureaucracies which distribute the funds. Too often these bureaucracies have not even attempted to understand the human problems that they are supposedly solving. This is understandable because, of course, these bureaucracies have been tremendously overburdened with work. The people staffing them have been badly paid and there is little status. Many who live day to day with human misery tend to establish a mechanism of self-defense. They reject personal involvement in their casework fearing that they will be overwhelmed and unable to function.

For all of these reasons, the welfare system is under heavy attack. It has never really been adequate to the needs in any country. We cannot predict what will replace the welfare system. Clearly the capitalist system must, in order to survive, come up with some other way of overcoming its problems of poverty, some way of ensuring the equality of opportunity that is basic to a successful capitalist system. There are, of course, no easy solutions to any of these problems, but solutions must be found.

Democracy and socialism

The fundamental assumption underlying democratic socialism is that participation in political decision making should be extended to economic decision making. This basic assumption is not always clearly stated, but it is the single most important argument put forth by democratic socialists because it most solidly places them within democratic theory. Democratic socialists argue that, since the economy and politics are so closely intertwined, the voters should be in a position to control their economic futures through the government they elect. Democratic socialists also argue that the democratic capitalist system gives too much power to individuals and groups that cannot be checked at the polls. They contend that these individuals and groups must be placed under the direct control of the people through the electoral process.

If one assumes that citizens should control their political lives and contribute to political decision making, it is only a short step to the democratic socialist argument that citizens should have some say in economic decision making. There is no question that economic decisions in connection with, for example, a steel industry have tremendous impact on an entire country. Therefore, democratic socialists argue that there must be some means for the people to have a check on such economic decisions. However, what economic decisions are significant in this sense? What industries are key industries for a national economy? Democratic socialists argue that these questions should be answered by the elected representatives of the people, and that the answers are likely to vary from country to country. In addition, the forms of governmental control and regulation and extent of public ownership of industry are likely to vary from country to country, depending upon the decisions made by the elected representatives of the people checked, of course, at the polls by the people themselves.

Another argument for democratic socialism, perhaps the most appealing one, is what one might call the humanitarian argument. Democratic socialists contend that the capitalist system has failed to solve the fundamental problems of poverty, disease, and so forth, that face a country. They say that capitalism may be capable of solving these problems but, since the economic decision makers are not checked by the needs and desires of people as a whole, they have ignored these basic problems. Democratic socialists argue that only when the economic system is controlled by the people will solutions to these problems be possible. They say that the capitalist is too concerned with profit. Therefore, they say that democratic socialism is essential if we are going to overcome the most basic problems of society, since only under democratic socialism can the people demand solutions.

The difference in means is the most obvious distinction between the two systems. Democratic socialism can be loosely characterized as follows:

1. Much property held by the public through the democratically elected government, including all the major industries, utilities, and transportation.

2. A limit on the accumulation of private property.
3. Governmental regulation of the economy.
4. An extensive welfare system.

Democratic socialist systems in practice vary considerably from country to country, particularly in the degree to which the industries, utilities, transportation, and so forth, are directly owned by the government. In some countries, all of these are governmentally owned. In others only specific parts of industrial complexes are owned by the government. For example, in Britain not all of the major industries are governmentally owned —some are in private hands and some are owned by the government.

When we say that much property is held by the public, this refers to property that is crucial to the functioning of the economic system, such as transportation, steel, mining, and so forth. It does not mean that there is no private property. Private property is still held by the individual in personal belongings, housing, and most small businesses, and in some cases large corporations. Some democratic socialists, theorists, and systems do not limit the amount of private property that can be held by an individual but others do. There is no necessity within democratic socialist theory for such limitations. On the other hand, most approaches suggest some degree of redistribution of income that would justify limiting private property.

The government of a democratic socialist system clearly will regulate that part of the economy that it does not own directly. This regulation is designed to ensure that the businesses that are privately owned are operated in the best interests of the society as a whole, rather than simply for private profit. This point illuminates the ethos of democratic socialism as opposed to democratic capitalism. Democratic socialism is concerned with society as a whole. The word *socialism* refers to *social* theories rather than to theories oriented toward the individual, and *democratic socialism* stresses the public as the center of political and economic power. More clearly than almost any other theory, democratic socialist theory is concerned with the people as a whole. Democratic capitalism is a theory concerned with the individual and only secondarily with society or the public as a whole. This is not to say, of course, that either democratic socialism or democratic capitalism forgets the other side. It simply illustrates the emphasis of each theory.

This emphasis leads to basic differences between the two theories. Both are concerned with the individual. Both are concerned with the welfare of all within the society. But democratic socialism stresses individual equality and the society as a whole; democratic capitalism stresses the economic individual.

In addition to the democratic proposition proclaimed in the basic assumption above, the theory suggests that liberty cannot be maintained without some minimal economic equality. This argument resembles that of the modern democratic capitalist for the welfare state as a means of securing equality of opportunity, but it is broader in that it demands more than equality of opportunity. The democratic socialist says that neither the right to vote nor any other form of liberty is possible unless every person within the society is economically secure. If insecure, he or she will be incapable of exercising personal liberty. Such economic security can be ensured only through an extensive welfare system.

This extensive welfare system of democratic socialism shares the same problems as the welfare system under democratic capitalism. But there are two major differences: the welfare system of democratic socialism covers far more and sometimes derives from different financing. Of course both systems are financed directly from taxes, but in the democratic socialist system, profit from the nationalized industries (i.e., the industries owned by the government), can be channeled into the system. This, of course, does not mitigate the problems of any welfare system, as we noted when discussing democratic capitalism. They still exist and they must be solved.

The typical democratic socialist welfare system includes an extensive medical care system that either is free or is provided at minimal cost. This usually includes prenatal care for mothers, dental care, and eye examinations, in addition to the more typical health services. An obvious practical rationale for an extensive health system is that a healthy individual can contribute more to society than can a sick one. Therefore, it is certainly to the advantage of the society as a whole to ensure the health of all. This is, of course, the fundamental rationale of any welfare system—that an individual who is maintained at the minimum level of life can contribute to society. The welfare system is also designed to take care of those who have already made a contribution to society and are now incapable of caring for themselves. Thus, the welfare system provides money for food, housing, and the other minimum necessities.

But the bureaucracy running the system presents one of the greatest problems for democratic socialism. Whether in business or in government, it is difficult for a bureaucracy to be as well informed or as responsive to the needs of the people or the industry it serves as would be ideal. Thus, many argue that a large bureaucratic system threatens the public control that the whole democratic socialist system is trying to preserve, because the bureaucracy is not directly responsible to the people. In essence, the democratic socialist system replaces those individuals and groups in the democratic capitalist system who are not held directly accountable to the people with a bureaucracy that is not held directly accountable to the people. Usually the bureaucracy is composed in large part of unchanging full-time employees who may at times follow policies of their own rather than of the political leaders.

Therefore, democratic socialism at times faces the same problems for which it criticizes democratic capitalism. Still, the democratic socialist would argue that, through their elected representatives, people do have control over the bureaucracy and that the government can immediately change the operations of the bureaucracy when it becomes cumbersome or ineffectual.

In many countries both democratic socialist and democratic capitalist, there has been instituted an *ombudsman* (the word derives from a Swedish term for deputy or representative) who hears complaints about the bureaucracy, investigates them and often makes sure that their causes are corrected. Such a person fills an obvious need because most bureaucracies are unwieldly, operate inefficiently, and find it hard to take individual differences into account. Actually, the operation of the ombudsman has revealed that the majority of complaints were either ill-founded or derived from a minority of incompetent bureaucrats and were easily remedied.

Thus, democratic countries have begun to recognize the problem of the bureaucracy and attempt to correct it. At the same time, there may be some protection for liberty in the relatively independent nature of the bureaucracy. Thus, one bureaucracy may force another bureaucracy to respond better than it would on its own. A case comes to mind in which a university professor from the United States was invited to Canada by a group to give a speech. An immigration official refused the professor entry into Canada, seemingly because of his pacifist views. The Canadian Broadcasting Company picked up the story and brought it to the attention of the government. Ultimately, the professor was allowed to speak and, rather than addressing a very small number of people in the original group, spoke over nationwide television. This illustrates how two bureaucracies, the immigration bureau and the Canadian Broadcasting Company, by coming into conflict, actually helped to protect the liberty and the freedom of the college professor to speak. Of course, this should not have been necessary in the first place but, given the problems that we have noted in bureaucracies, perhaps it is a hopeful sign.

Finally, the similarities between democratic capitalism and democratic socialism are much greater than are the differences. The differences center on the point of governmental or public ownership of the majority of the important segments of the economy as opposed to private ownership. This central difference is, of course, important and is the focus of the major disagreements between the democratic capitalists and the democratic socialists. Related to this central difference is one that should be emphasized—the conflicting concern with economic freedom in democratic capitalism and economic equality in democratic socialism. The other differences, though, seem to be of degree rather than of kind. The extent of the welfare system in democratic socialism is nowhere prohibited by democratic capitalist theory. The bureaucracies of the two are facing similar problems in the world today. Both democratic socialism and democratic capitalism have produced affluence, but with affluence, poverty. And the governments of various countries are attempting to overcome poverty within the dictates of either the capitalist or the socialist system. So far neither one has been very successful.

CONSERVATISM

The most bothersome problem in discussing conservatism and liberalism is their tendency to differ from place to place and time to time. Conservatism is interested, obviously, in conserving something, but it is difficult to generalize about what it wants to conserve because a Canadian conservative will emphasize something different from a Japanese or Swedish conservative. In addition, a conservative in the United States in the last half of the 20th century does not believe the same things that a U.S. conservative in 1890 did.

Given this, we must attempt to avoid the time and place limitations and find a characterization of conservatism that will be broad enough to fit conservatism at a reasonable number of times and places, at the same time, not so general as to be meaningless.

Conservatism within democracy today may best be characterized as follows:

1. Resistance to change.
2. Reverence for tradition and a distrust of human reason.
3. Rejection of the use of government to improve the human condition—ambivalence regarding governmental activity.
4. Favoring individual freedom but willing to limit freedom.
5. Antiegalitarian—distrust of human nature.

In an essay entitled, "Why I Am Not a Conservative," F. A. Hayek wrote that "Conservatism proper is a legitimate, probably necessary, and certainly widespread attitude of opposition to drastic change."[28] Although his point is correct, it is too specific. Conservatives not only oppose "drastic change," as he says, but they also are hesitant about any change. As Jay A. Sigler put it, "The conservative does not oppose change, but he does resist it."[29]

Of course, there are exceptions to this generalization as there are to every generalization about conservatism or liberalism. Conservatives *resist* and question change, particularly

---

[28] F. A. Hayek, "Why I Am Not a Conservative," in *The Constitution of Liberty* (London: Routledge & Kegan Paul, 1960), p. 397.

[29] Jay A. Sigler, "Introduction," in Sigler, ed., *The Conservative Tradition in American Thought* (New York: Capricorn Books, 1969), p. 13.

change for the sake of change since they are wary of social experimentation. They do not unthinkingly oppose change; they *resist* it and question it. They believe that something that has worked, even if not very well, is better than something untried and unknown.

Point two, a "reverence for tradition," is composed of a number of subsidiary points. They include traditional moral standards, religion (with very few exceptions), and generally the assumption that the longer an institution has existed the more likely it is to be worth preserving. This shows the conservative's basic distrust of reason as a means of improving humanity's lot. Conservatives do not reject reason completely, but they would rather trust tradition. Note also how closely connected points one and two are—honoring tradition entails resistance to change.

This point is quite simple and clear-cut. The only really complicating factor is that conservatives (and liberals) change over time regarding the specifics they wish to preserve. The world changes and conservatives change with it. They do not want to conserve all the past; they do want to conserve what they see as best in the past.

Point three presents the major dilemma in conservative thought. On the whole conservatives believe that governmental power should be reduced and that individuals should make their own way in the world. (Note the similarity to traditional capitalism.) But there is an ambivalence here. Governmental power to support the traditional moral standards and limit an individual's freedom regarding them is perfectly acceptable to conservatives. This is because conservatives believe that "genuinely ordered freedom is the only sort of liberty worth having: freedom made possible by order within the soul and order within the state."[30]

But we must not overstate the case. Conservatives basically reject the use of government to improve the human condition. They do this because (1) they are convinced that the use of government does not necessarily help to improve the human condition, and (2) they believe that people left alone can do a

[30] Russell Kirk, "Prescription, Authority, and Ordered Freedom," in Frank S. Meyer, ed., *What Is Conservatism?* (New York: Holt, Rinehart & Winston, 1964), p. 24.

better job. The first point is the key one. It asserts that the use of government for social betterment will actually produce the opposite. People will, according to most conservatives, come to rely on government and lose the ability to help themselves.

Conservatives have held this position very consistently. Edmund Burke writing in the 18th century held it; Bernard Bosanquet writing at the beginning of this century held it; and modern conservatives, such as Russell Kirk still hold it. Persons of the better sort will be hurt by governmental help; the poorer sort will not be helped.

Conservatives believe that there are people who are better than other people and who, therefore, should be given greater due in society. "Aye, men are created different; and a government which ignores this law becomes an unjust government, for it sacrifices nobility to mediocrity; it pulls down the aspiring natures to gratify the inferior natures."[31] And this is precisely why conservatives are ambivalent about both government and individual freedom.

"The conservative accepts as natural the differences which separate men. Class, intelligence, nationality, and race make men different."[32] This recognition of differences sometimes implies superiority or inferiority, but it does not necessarily do so. The recognition states that inferiority and superiority exist, but it does not necessarily tie this to race, class, or sex.

These five are the basic defining characteristics of conservatism. Although the specifics do change, it would be pointless to try to trace out the details here because too many writers get lost in the changes that take place in conservatism (and liberalism) and forget the fairly simple principles that characterize both of them and that do not change much over time.[33]

LIBERALISM

Liberalism has a complex history, as does conservatism, and it has played many roles in Western thought. It is difficult to

---

[31] Ibid., p. 34.

[32] Sigler, *The Conservative Tradition*, p. 13.

[33] For further reference, see ibid.; Peter Viereck, *Conservatism: From John Adams to Churchill* (Princeton, N.J.: D. Van Nostrand Co., 1956); and Robert Lindsay Schuettinger, ed., *The Conservative Tradition in European Thought* (New York: G. P. Putnam's Sons, 1970).

pin down precisely because it has changed from time to time and place to place as much as conservatism has. As one scholar recently notes, "Rather than being a current manifestation of a long intellectual tradition, liberalism, as it is understood today, is largely a product of the twentieth century."[34] We can, though, clearly demonstrate its differences from conservatism.

Liberalism within democracy today can be characterized as follows:

1. Having a tendency to favor change.
2. Possessing faith in human reason.
3. Being willing to use government to improve the human condition.
4. Favoring individual freedom.
5. Being ambivalent regarding human nature.

Hubert H. Humphrey once wrote, "Liberals fully recognize that *change* is inevitable in the patterns of society and in the challenges which confront man."[35] Liberals generally believe that people should keep trying to improve society. Somewhat less optimistic about progress than it once was, liberalism still believes that beneficial change is possible. This change can come about through the conscious action of men and women, as unforeseen side effects of decisions, or through the operation of various social forces. But there will be change, and the liberal is convinced that it can be directed and controlled for human benefit.

They do not desire radical change that does away with the basic structure of the current system. On this point, the difference between liberalism and conservatism is more of degree than of kind. The liberals want more change and tend to favor social experimentation, but they want this only within the framework of the current political, legal, and economic systems. They are not radicals.[36]

[34] Walter E. Volkomer, "Introduction," in Volkomer, ed., *The Liberal Tradition in American Thought* (New York: Capricorn Books, 1969), p. 1. See the Suggested Readings at the end of the chapter for opposing interpretations.

[35] Hubert H. Humphrey, "Introduction," in Milton Viorst, *Liberalism: A Guide to Its Past, Present and Future in American Politics* (New York: Avon Books, 1963), p. vii. Emphasis in the original.

[36] Arnold S. Kaufman argues that this is changing. See his *The Radical Liberal: New Man in American Politics* (New York: Atherton Press, 1968).

Change is welcomed because liberals trust the possibilities of human reason to derive solutions to human problems. This faith in the potential of reason is the key to the liberal credo—only with such faith could they accept the use of governmental power to help improve the human condition. This faith is not a naïve, unquestioning faith, but it assumes that social experimentation is valid and that it is better to use such powers as we have to control change than to simply allow change to come and control us.

Liberals contend that people must and can be helped to live a better life and fulfill individual potential. Conservatives believe just the opposite—helping people will make it impossible for them to fulfill their potential as individuals. Liberals argue that people, though capable of reason and reasoned action, are often caught in situations where self-help, although not impossible, is difficult and that the government should step in and help. This assistance, far from injuring people, can (not will) give them the impetus to do more for themselves. Their assumption is that, although not everyone will respond, it is better to attempt to help than to do nothing. In contemporary society, they believe, only government is in a position to help.

Liberals believe that this help, through governmental activity, will lead to greater individual freedom. They argue that a person, once relieved of some basic problems, can enlarge his or her sphere of activity and improve both life and mind. Still, liberals are somewhat ambivalent about human nature. They contend that most problems derive from impersonal social and economic forces acting on humanity, and that human reason can solve the problems, but not an unaided human being.

The tradition of liberalism most strongly stresses individual freedom. The term *liberalism* is closely related to liberty, and the emphasis on liberty has been a major thread in all liberal thought. Liberals believe that the individual must be protected and encouraged to develop his or her potential.

The role of the government thus is limited—it cannot invade the rights and freedoms of the individual. Human beings will err, but liberals have always believed that error is far better than the suppression of error. This belief follows from the belief in the value and inevitability of change. If change is good and will always occur, today's error may be tomorrow's truth.

Liberalism and conservatism are both primarily attitudes toward change within the democratic tradition, resting uneasily between reaction and revolution. Too often attempts are made to transform them into major ideologies with rigidly defined beliefs. This is clearly an error. They do not have these clear-cut beliefs except briefly in response to current problems.

CURRENT ISSUES

All ideologies are undergoing constant change, sometimes drastic, sometimes minor. Today democracy of all kinds and varieties appears to be somewhat in flux. There is a constantly growing concern with equality and governmental activities to achieve that equality coupled with a growing distrust of government's ability to provide solutions without unreasonable limitations on individual freedom. In a sense both liberalism and conservatism appear to be becoming more alike, and this is happening in both democratic capitalist and democratic socialist countries.

A central issue today is the question of privacy, how large is the area of negative liberty where the individual should simply be left alone. The debate includes questions ranging from wiretapping to sexual morality and so-called victimless crimes such as prostitution.

Thus the greatest issues for democracy today are simply modifications of the basic questions, to what extent can meaningful participation be provided in our complex modern civilization and how can we foster both freedom and equality and make them realities that are achieved rather than goals that are always slightly out of reach.

SUGGESTED READINGS

The principles of democracy

Adler, Mortimer J.   *The Idea of Freedom; A Dialectical Examination of the Conceptions of Freedom.* Garden City, N.Y.: Doubleday & Co., 1958.

Bay, Christian.   *The Structure of Freedom.* Stanford, Calif.: Stanford University Press, 1958.

Birch, A. H.   *Representation.* London: Pall Mall Press, 1971.

Braybrooke, David.   *Three Tests for Democracy, Personal Rights, Human Welfare, Collective Preference*. New York: Random House, 1968.

Christophersen, Jens A.   *The Meaning of Democracy as Used in European Ideologies; An Historical Study in Political Language*. Oslo: Universitetsforlaget, 1966.

Cohen, Carl.   *Democracy*. Athens, Ga.: University of Georgia Press, 1971.

Cranston, Maurice.   *What Are Human Rights?* London: Bodley Head, 1973.

Dahl, Robert A.   *A Preface to Democratic Theory*. Chicago: University of Chicago Press, 1956.

The Federalist Papers.   Any edition.

Hallowell, John H.   *The Moral Foundations of Democracy*. Chicago: University of Chicago Press, 1954.

Kristol, Irving.   *On the Democratic Idea in America*. New York: Harper & Row, 1972.

Lively, Jack.   *Democracy*. Oxford: Basil Blackwell, 1975.

Macpherson, C. B.   *The Real World of Democracy*. Oxford, Eng.: Clarendon Press, 1966.

———.   *Democratic Theory: Essays in Retrieval*. Oxford, Eng.: Clarendon Press, 1973.

Mayo, Henry B.   *An Introduction to Democratic Theory*. New York: Oxford University Press, 1960.

Oppenheim, Felix E.   *Dimensions of Freedom; An Analysis*. New York: St. Martin's Press, 1961.

Pitkin, Hanna Fenichal.   *The Concept of Representation*. Berkeley, Calif.: University of California Press, 1967.

Plamenatz, John.   *Democracy and Illusion; An Examination of Certain Aspects of Modern Democratic Theory*. London: Longmans, 1973.

Rawls, John.   *A Theory of Justice*. Oxford, Eng.: Clarendon Press, 1972.

Rees, John.   *Equality*. London: Pall Mall Press, 1971.

Sartori, Giovanni.   *Democratic Theory*. New York: Frederick A. Praeger, 1965.

Simon, Yves.   *Philosophy of Democratic Government*. Chicago: University of Chicago Press, 1951.

Democratic capitalism

Berle, Adolf A., Jr.   *The 20th Century Capitalist Revolution*. New York: Harcourt Brace & Co., 1954.

Chase, Harold W., and Dolan, Paul.   *The Case for Democratic Capitalism*. New York: Thomas Y. Crowell, 1964.

Friedman, Milton.   *Capitalism and Freedom*. Chicago: University of Chicago Press, 1962.

Tipple, John.   *The Capitalist Revolution: A History of American Social Thought 1890–1919*. New York: Pegasus, 1970.

Wright, David McCord.   *Capitalism*. Chicago: Henry Regnery, 1962.

————.   *Democracy and Progress*. New York: Macmillan Co., 1948.

Democratic socialism

Crosland, C. A. R.   *The Future of Socialism*. New York: Schocken Books, 1963.

————.   *Socialism Now and Other Essays*. London: Jonathan Cape, 1974.

Crossman, R. H. S., ed.   *New Fabian Essays*. London: Turnstile Press, 1952.

————.   *The Politics of Socialism*. New York: Atheneum, 1965.

Harrington, Michael.   *Socialism*. New York: Saturday Review Press, 1972.

Holland, Stuart.   *The Socialist Challenge*. London: Quartet Books, 1975.

Nove, Alec.   *Efficiency Criteria for Nationalised Industries*. London: George Allen & Unwin, 1974.

Paterson, William E., and Campbell, Ian.   *Social Democracy in Post-War Europe*. London: Macmillan & Co., 1974.

The Socialist Register.   New York: Monthly Review Press, 1964—.

Conservatism

Buckley, William F., ed.   *Did You Ever See a Dream Walking? American Conservative Thought in the Twentieth Century*. Indianapolis: Bobbs-Merrill, 1970.

Diggins, John P.   *Up From Communism; Conservative Odysseys in American Intellectual History*. New York: Harper & Row, 1976.

Goldsmith, M. M., and Hawkins, Michael.   "The New American Conservatism," *Political Studies*, vol. 20 (March 1972), pp. 60–78.

Hayek, Friedrich A.   *The Road to Serfdom*. Chicago: University of Chicago Press, 1944.

————.   *The Constitution of Liberty*. London: Routledge & Kegan Paul, 1960.

————.   *Studies in Philosophy, Politics and Economics*. Chicago: University of Chicago Press, 1967.

Holden, Matthew, Jr., ed.   *Varieties of Political Conservatism*. Beverly Hills, Calif.: Sage Publications, 1974.

Kendall, Willmoore.   *The Conservative Affirmation*. Chicago: Henry Regnery Co., 1954.

————, and Carey, George W.   "Towards a Definition of 'Conservatism,'" *Journal of Politics*, vol. 26 (May 1964), pp. 406–22.

Kirk, Russell.   *A Program for Conservatives.* Chicago: Henry Regnery Co., 1954.

――――.   *The Conservative Mind.* Rev. ed. Chicago: Henry Regnery Co., 1960.

Kolko, Gabriel.   *The Triumph of Conservatism; A Reinterpretation of American History, 1900–1916.* New York: Free Press, 1963.

Meyer, Frank S., ed.   *What Is Conservatism?* New York: Holt, Rinehart & Winston, 1964.

Nash, George H.   *The Conservative Intellectual in America Since 1945.* New York: Basic Books, 1976.

Rossiter, Clinton.   *Conservatism in America; The Thankless Persuasion.* 2d ed. rev. New York: Alfred A. Knopf, 1966.

Schuettinger, Robert Lindsay, ed.   *The Conservative Tradition in European Thought.* New York: G. P. Putnam's Sons, 1970.

Sigler, Jay A., ed.   *The Conservative Tradition in American Thought.* New York: Capricorn Books, 1969.

Smith, Dean.   *Conservatism: A Guide to Its Past, Present and Future in American Politics.* New York: Avon Books, 1963.

Viereck, Peter.   *Conservatism: From John Adams to Churchill.* Princeton, N.J.: D. Van Nostrand Co., 1956.

Liberalism

Cumming, Robert Denoon.   *Human Nature and History. A Study of the Development of Liberal Thought.* 2 vols. Chicago: University of Chicago Press, 1969.

De Ruggiero, Guido.   *The History of European Liberalism.* Trans. R. G. Collingwood. Boston: Beacon Press, 1959.

Girvetz, Harry K.   *The Evolution of Liberalism.* New York: Collier Books, 1963.

Kaufman, Arnold S.   *The Radical Liberal; New Man in American Politics.* New York: Atherton Press, 1968.

Laski, Harold J.   *The Rise of European Liberalism: An Essay in Interpretation.* London: George Allen & Unwin, 1936.

Minogue, Kenneth.   *The Liberal Mind.* New York: Vintage Books, 1963.

Schapiro, J. Salwyn.   *Liberalism: Its Meaning and History.* Princeton, N.J.: D. Van Nostrand Co., 1958.

Sidorsky, David.   *The Liberal Tradition in European Thought.* New York: G. P. Putnam's Sons, 1970.

Spitz, David.   *Essays in the Liberal Idea of Freedom.* Tucson, Ariz.: University of Arizona Press, 1964.

Viorst, Milton.   *Liberalism; A Guide to Its Past, Present and Future in American Politics.* New York: Avon Books, 1963.

Volkomer, Walter E., ed.   *The Liberal Tradition in American Thought.* New York: Capricorn Books, 1969.

4

Communism

Among the major ideologies today, the most misunderstood and feared in the United States is communism. Communism is the most noticeable alternative to the democratic ideology. Communism is the official ideology of the Soviet Union and China, the most obvious military threats to the United States. But the fear of communism has been common, for most of this century, so that the current military situation is not a sufficient explanation for that fear.

Although, it is not the purpose here to attempt any thoroughgoing analysis of the causes of this fear, it may help us understand some facts about communism if some of the more obvious reasons are described briefly. As already mentioned, one cause is the military posture of the world today. A second reason might be that communism is opposed to capitalism and Western democracy, and Communist leaders argue that capitalism will inevitably collapse. A third might be a belief in the Communist desire to conquer the entire world, or at least to attempt to cause revolution in non-Communist countries. The whole cold war relationship between the United States and Communist countries with its missile crisis, periodic hot wars, and its period of intense hatred in the McCarthy[1] era are also

---

[1] Joseph R. McCarthy (1909–57), U.S. Senator from Wisconsin 1946–57, was noted for his intense campaign against alleged Communists. This culminated in the Army–McCarthy hearings which were televised in 1954. McCarthy was censured by the Senate that year.

part of the picture. A final reason might be found in a tendency to reject any group that challenges basic contemporary institutions.

There is much talk about the "Communist conspiracy" and Communist attempts to control the world. Although some justification for these beliefs can be found in Communist writings, they seem to represent a misunderstanding of contemporary communism. Based on the writings of Karl Marx (1818–83) and Friedrich Engels (1820–95),[2] as developed by Nikolai Lenin (real name: Vladimir Ilich Ulyanov: 1870–1924) and others, communism is now the official ideology of two of the largest and most powerful countries of the world, the USSR and China, and a number of smaller countries around them, as well as Cuba in the Western hemisphere.

Many people make the error of simply equating the ideas of contemporary communism with those of Marx and Engels. Although it is impossible to understand communism fully as it is today without grasping the central ideas developed by Marx, Engels, and Lenin, the differences between their ideas and contemporary communism are great, and in this chapter some of the similarities and differences will be examined. There are many similar errors which distort the meaning of both Marx and Engels and contemporary communism. One of the most common of these is to view communism as being completely monolithic, allowing no national or even personal differences. Although it would undoubtedly be impossible for such total conformity to ever exist, and although it could not be further from the truth, belief in it is still widely held. The changes in Eastern Europe point to two major ways in which this view of communism as a completely monolithic system are incorrect. In the first place, the attempts of a variety of the Eastern European countries, such as Czechoslovakia, to change their systems internally while still remaining a Communist country illustrate that there are important national differences among Commu-

---

[2] For our purposes Marx and Engels can be treated as essentially the same. For a more sophisticated discussion, see Friedrich Engels, *Selected Writings*, ed. W. O. Henderson (Baltimore: Penguin Books, 1967), and Fritz Nova, *Friedrich Engels; His Contributions to Political Theory* (London: Vision Press, 1967). Also see Heinrich Gemkow et al., *Friedrich Engels: A Biography* (Dresden: Verlag Zeit im Bild, 1972).

nist countries. This same point should also be clear from the split between Moscow and Peking or the split in previous years between Russia and Yugoslavia. From all of this it should be sufficiently clear that neither communism nor the Communist nations are any more monolithic than democracy and the democratic nations. But it should be equally apparent that the Soviet Union is strongly opposed to these developments and tries to discourage them or forcibly stop them, usually with some success.

Since communism is so widespread today, it is obviously important to understand it. In order to do so, it is essential to look first at the philosophic basis of communism as found in the thought of Karl Marx and Friedrich Engels and then to turn to the developments and changes made in this basic doctrine by such thinkers as Lenin, Mao Tse-tung, Khrushchev, and others.

ALIENATION—THE YOUNG MARX

There has been considerable debate over the past few years regarding similarities and differences between Marx's early writings and his later works. Although Marx scholars will be debating this issue for years, and we will learn a great deal from the debate, at the moment it is possible to tentatively conclude that there are significant areas in which the later writings seem to develop from the early ones.[3]

The basic concept in the so-called early writings is that of *alienation,* a term that has been greatly overused in the past few years. The concept refers to a relationship between two or more people or entities, or even parts of oneself in which one is cut off from, alien to, outside the other.[4] For Marx it meant something specific. In capitalism, for reasons that will become more apparent later, individuals become cut off from, out of tune with themselves, their families and friends, and their work.

---

[3] Here I follow David McLellan, *Karl Marx; His Life and Thought* (New York: Harper & Row, Publishers, 1973). See also, Gajo Petrovic, *Marx in the Mid-Twentieth Century; A Yugoslav Philosopher Considers Karl Marx's Writings* (Garden City, N.Y.: Anchor Books, 1967), particularly pp. 31–51.

[4] It has been a major theme in modern literature with works such as Albert Camus' *The Stranger* (1942), Jean–Paul Sartre's *Nausea* (1938) and *No Exit* (1945), and Samuel Beckett's *Waiting for Godot* (1952), picturing, among other things, men and women cut off from the world and themselves.

They are not and cannot be whole, fully developed human beings in a capitalist society.[5] Marx's vision of the effects of capitalism was at the base of his entire critique of capitalism and informed his later writing.

The new Marxists of Eastern Europe see that most of these problems have not been solved by the introduction of socialism, at least not as it now exists. Therefore, they are returning to the early writings of Marx for inspiration in attacking the real, human problems that exist today, under socialism. They find that Marx's concern with the day-to-day problems of real people help them to criticize the current scene, and they hope thereby to reform socialism as it now functions.[6]

At the same time they have been reading the existentialists, such as Jean-Paul Sartre and Albert Camus. Most of the writings of the existentialists depict modern humans cut off from or alienated from nature (Sartre's novel *Nausea* [1938] although meaning something very different by nature than did Marx), themselves (Camus' play *Caligula* [1944]), or the rest of humanity (almost all Camus' writings, particularly the novels *The Stranger* [1942] and *The Fall* [1956]).

The concerns of the young Marx and the contemporary existentialists are the same and even some of the terms are similar, but there are important differences.[7] For our purposes, however, it is more important to note the meeting of the concerns of the young Marx and the contemporary existentialists in the writings of Eastern European Marxists such as Adam Schaff, Lezek Kolakowski, and to a lesser extent, Georg Lukacs and others.[8] Among these writers and a growing number of younger

---

[5] For an extended commentary, see Istvan Meszaros, *Marx's Theory of Alienation* (London: Merlin Press, 1970); Bertell Ollman, *Alienation*, 2d ed. (Cambridge: Cambridge University Press, 1976); and Adam Schaff, "Alienation as a Social and Philosophical Problem," *Social Praxis*, 3, #1–2 (1975), pp. 7–26.

[6] A good introduction is Richard T. De George, *The New Marxism; Soviet and East European Marxism Since 1956* (New York: Pegasus, 1968).

[7] Since we are primarily concerned with communism, a detailed analysis of these similarities and differences is inappropriate here. The interested reader should consult Raymond Aron, *Marxism and the Existentialists* (New York: Simon & Schuster, 1969); Wilfrid Desan, *The Marxism of Jean-Paul Sartre* (Garden City, N.Y.: Anchor Books, 1966); and Walter Odajnyk, *Marxism and Existentialism* (Garden City, N.Y.: Anchor Books, 1965).

[8] See, for example, Adam Schaff, *Marxism and the Human Individual*, ed. Robert S. Cohen, and trans. Olgierd Wojtasiewicz (New York: McGraw-Hill

thinkers, one finds the early humanist Marx resurrected. They argue that Marxism must reject many of its own dogmas and return to a concern for the individual human being. They still accept communism; they still reject capitalism. They still argue that capitalism systematically degrades humanity and that only a system of communism is capable of achieving a society that will truly free human beings.

They are not rejecting the general lines of their heritage, but are trying to rebuild a new version of Marx's original vision. They are saying that communism must give more scope to the individual; that it must recognize that the goal has not yet been fully realized; that the goal must be explored further; and that short-term reform now is highly desirable.

The central difference that some scholars see between the early writings of Marx and his later writings are found more in emphasis than in a development of entirely new concepts. The major change is that the focus on alienation found in the early works is replaced by a focus on the social relations of production. Also, Marx tends gradually to drop the theory of subsistence wages.

MARX'S CRITIQUE OF CAPITALISM

The Marxian analysis of society and the forces operating in it is directed at a commentary on, and condemnation of, industrial capitalism. Marx attributed most of the ills of contemporary society to the capitalist system and its product, the class struggle. There is no question that there were many evils inherent in developing industrialism, and certainly Marx was not the only one to point them out. His comments on contemporary society are interesting, though, because they indicate a great deal about Marx and the way he viewed the world. In addition, both Marxian communism and contemporary communism are

Book Co., 1970); Lezek Kolakowski, *Toward a Marxist Humanism; Essays on the Left Today,* trans. Jane Zielonko Peel (New York: Grove Press, 1968); Georg Lukacs, *History and Class Consciousness; Studies in Marxist Dialectics,* trans. Rodney Livingstone (Cambridge, Mass.: M.I.T. Press, 1971); Mihailo Marković, *From Affluence to Praxis; Philosophy and Social Criticism* (Ann Arbor, Mich.: University of Michigan Press, 1974); and Svetozar Stojanovic, *Between Ideals and Reality; A Critique of Socialism and Its Future,* trans. Gerson S. Sher (New York: Oxford University Press, 1973).

attempts to solve the problems of industrialism. Much of the thrust and appeal of Marxism is found in these criticisms of the industrial system. Therefore, an understanding of communism is impossible without a careful consideration of these criticisms.

Since for Marx economics is the foundation of the entire social system, Marx's economic criticisms should be considered first. The primary points in Marxian economics are the *labor theory of value*, the doctrine of *subsistence wages*, and the theory of *surplus value*. Generally, Marx used value in the sense of real costs in labor. Nothing else was considered. In other words, the value, not the price, of any manufactured object was based on the amount of labor time consumed in producing it. This is the labor theory of value. A man has to work a certain number of hours or days to produce enough to provide himself with a living. Marx assumed that the capitalist would pay the man only enough to keep him alive, a subsistence wage. Marx made this assumption because:

1. There was a surplus of laborers and there was no need to pay more.
2. He could not conceive of the capitalist paying more than absolutely necessary.
3. He assumed that the capitalist would be faced with a series of economic crises which would make it impossible for the capitalist to pay more.

In addition, Marx believed that the profit of the capitalist was taken from the amount produced over and above the wages paid the worker. This is the theory of surplus value and can be used to explain more fully the doctrine of subsistence wages. As capitalists replaced workers with machines, they would have to reduce wages to keep up their rate of profit, since profit came only from surplus value extracted from labor.

Hence, Marx's major economic criticisms of the society in which he lived turned on the exploitation of the majority, the proletariat or workers by the minority, the bourgeoisie or capitalists. His concern was not purely economic but was centered on the extent to which the system kept proletarians from ever fulfilling their potentials as individuals. It was impossible for them to improve themselves in any way. They were denied education and were thus kept from any real understanding of their deplorable position.

The state was the tool of the dominant class, the bourgeoisie, and was used by them to suppress violently any attempt by the proletariat to better themselves. It should be kept in mind that the state to Marx and many other radical theorists of the day referred to all those official persons, such as the police, the army, and so forth, that could be and were used to suppress the workers. In addition, Marx contended that as long as the bourgeoisie was the dominant class, the government would be its tool and could not be made responsive to the needs of other classes. The state or the government was always viewed by Marx as the tool of the dominant class, whichever class that might be, and it would so remain as long as there was more than one class. The state, for many radicals of the period and for certain radicals today, is the epitome of evil, the symbol of all that is bad about society. This is particularly true among the anarchists, and will be discussed in detail in the chapter on anarchism. It is also true of Marx and some of Marx's followers, particularly prior to Lenin. This notion probably developed because so often the state as manifested in the bureaucracy, in the police, and in the army represents all the forces that the workers see as opposed to their demands. The history of the labor movement in the United States, for example, illustrates frequent use of the police, the army, and such institutions as the National Guard to put down strikes, and, in general, to oppose the labor movement.[9] It is easy to see, then, why the state could come to symbolize all those forces opposed to the worker or even to change itself. Thus, Marx's ultimate utopia, Full Communism, has no state. And in this he is similar to the anarchists.

The religious system was also in the hands of the bourgeoisie, and Marx held that it was used to convince the proletariat that if they obeyed the state and their bosses they would be rewarded in another life. This is what Marx meant by his famous statement that religion is the opium of the people. The prole-

---

[9] For studies from differing viewpoints, see John R. Commons et al., *History of Labor in the United States,* 4th ed. (New York: Kelly, 1966); and Louis Adamic, *Dynamite; The Story of Class Violence in America,* rev. ed. (New York: Viking Press, 1934).

tariat was lulled into accepting their way of life by the vision of heaven. This life might well be harsh, but, if they just stood it for a brief time, they would be rewarded in the next life. Marx felt that this kept the workers from actively seeking to change the system. In this way, the religious system was a major focus of Marx's criticisms of contemporary society. He saw what he believed to be the superstition and hocus-pocus of religion used by the dominant class, the bourgeoisie, to hold the proletariat in its downtrodden position. Thus, Marx made many scathing attacks on the religious system of his day and argued that the future society in which the proletariat would rule would have no need for religion. It should also be noted that Marx's materialist position was diametrically opposed to any idea of religion.

The state and the religious system were both part of what Marx called the superstructure. They were not fundamental economic structures of society. Essentially, they were a reflection of the property relations and would change as these property relations changed. Thus, as the class antagonisms were overcome during the dictatorship of the proletariat both the state and religion would begin to disappear.

The capitalist system degraded workers in all of their relationships. Since they had to fight constantly against others of their class for bare subsistence, they could never hope to establish any sort of valid relationship with another person. For example, Marx wrote bitterly of the effect that capitalism had on marriage and the family. To Marx, the family system of his day was a repetition of the class struggle. The husband symbolized the bourgeoisie, the wife, the proletariat. The contemporary marriage system under capitalism was monogamy supplemented by adultery and prostitution, and it could not change until capitalism ceased to exist. The contemporary marriage system had originated as an institution of private property at about the same time that private property in land and goods had originated. It developed in order to ensure that a man's property would be handed on to his sons. The only way this could be done was to endow the sons of one woman with a particular legal status. This in no way limited the man's relationships with other women; it supposedly limited the wife's relationships with other men. In practice, as shown by adultery, this latter proscription did not work. It failed because of what Marx called "individual sex-love." He believed that sometime after the development of monogamous marriage, there developed the tendency to find one sex-love partner and no other. This could, of course, occur after marriage, and it explained the existence of adultery. But, as will be seen later, it also provided Marx with the basis for the true monogamous marriage that would develop after the revolution.[10]

PHILOSOPHICAL BASIS—MATERIALISM

There are a few highly theoretical points that must be grasped in order to understand the outlook of communism, and because they are so complicated, we will discuss them in detail. The basis of Marx's philosophy is found in the influence of the conditions of life on humans. Although Marx did not develop the basis of this notion thoroughly himself, he once spelled out in capsule form the fundamental thesis, saying that it "served as the guiding thread in my studies." Although the jargon is a bit difficult to follow, it is best to have this statement in Marx's own words, and it will become clearer later.

> In the social production of their means of existence men enter into definite, necessary relations which are independent of their will, productive relationships which correspond to a definite state of development of their material productive forces. The aggregate of these productive relationships constitutes the economic structure of society, the real basis on which a juridical and political superstructure arises, and to which definite forms of social consciousness correspond. The mode of production of the material means of existence conditions the whole process of social, political, and intellectual life. It is not the consciousness of men that determines their existence, but, on the contrary, it is their social condition that determines their consciousness. At a certain stage of their development the material productive forces of society come into contradiction with the existing productive relationships within which they had moved before. From forms of development of the productive forces these relationships are transformed into their fetters. Then an epoch of social revolu-

---

[10] Engels discussed the family at length in *The Origin of the Family, Private Property and the State* (New York: International Publishers, n.d.); for a recent Marxist commentary, see Juliet Mitchell, *Women's Estate* (Baltimore: Penguin Books, 1971).

tion opens. With the change in the economic foundation the whole vast superstructure is more or less rapidly transformed.[11]

I have thus quoted Marx because, as I hope to show, this remarkable passage thoroughly summarizes his basic ideas.

The most basic point, which is a truism today, is that the way people think is greatly affected by the way they live. It would be very difficult today to argue against this point. As was noted in the introduction, the whole process known as socialization is the means by which an individual gains the values of his or her particular society. The point we made there was that an individual by position in life, economically, socially, and so forth, and by family and religious background, educational experiences, and by such daily influences as the mass media, is presented with a picture, or a group of pictures, of the world that help to form his or her basic value system. In other words, the way an individual lives does quite clearly affect the way he or she thinks.

But the basic point that is generally accepted today is not quite the same as the point that Marx was making. Marx argued that the forms taken by law, religion, politics, aesthetics, philosophy, and so forth, which he called the *superstructure,* are determined by the economic structure and processes of society. The key word in the discussion by Marx is the word *determined.* While making the more general point about socialization above, we were careful to always say that the way a person lives *influences* or *helps* form the way he or she thinks. We did not say that these things *determined* the way he or she thinks. In addition, it should be noted that we were careful to talk in rather broad ways about the sorts of things that influence a person's developing value system. We did not, as Marx does, narrow our analysis to economics. Thus, it should be clear that Marx's position is not one that is generally accepted today at least in the non-Communist world, although no one would deny that economic factors are an important influence on one's value system. It is clear that economic factors do influence one's values and political behavior. Although the details of Marx's analysis are not generally accepted outside the Commu-

---

[11] Karl Marx, "Preface," in *A Contribution to the Critique of Political Economy,* trans. N. I. Stone (Chicago: Charles H. Kerr & Co., 1913), pp. 11–12.

nist world, his basic assumptions provide a way of looking at the world that leads to a much greater understanding of the forces that influence the development of man.

In its simplest form, these statements constitute Marx's materialism, and any understanding of the rest of his thought must be based on a thorough understanding of materialism. The basic notion, to which Marx adds certain complexities to be discussed later, is that all ideas, all thoughts, are reflections of matter or nature. Marx's position is that the material world around us, nature, determines the social, political, religious, and philosophical worlds. Marx took this idea and developed it by emphasizing economics until it formed the basis of his whole system.

In developing his materialist approach, Marx was attacking a school of German philosophy known as idealism. Its major exponent had been Georg Wilhelm Friedrich Hegel (1770–1831), and it was particularly against Hegel that Marx directed his attack. Hegel's ideas and the diverse influence they had on Marx is a complex subject and cannot be explored thoroughly here. But some attempt at explanation must be made because Hegel's influence on Marx, both in what he accepted and what he rejected, was so great. Suffice it to say that Hegel's basic proposition, from Marx's viewpoint, was the existence of an Absolute Spirit—sometimes Hegel called it God—that gradually revealed more and more of itself as higher and higher stages of freedom for man. In Hegel's philosophy the ideal and the material, or concrete, as he called it, were intimately connected, but not as cause and effect, as the material and the superstructure were related in Marx. For Hegel, the two were closely bound together, each influencing the other even though ultimately, the ideal was more important than the material.

Marx directed his main attack on Hegel at this idealism. As Marx put it, he turned Hegel on his head by emphasizing the material rather than the ideal. Marx, of course, stressed economic relationships in his definition of the material rather than physical nature or the like. For this reason, Marx has been called an economic determinist, but the idea of materialism is not quite that simple. By stressing the material, Marx is able to argue that his position is scientific (Marx's approach is often called scientific socialism)[12] because matter, the material, is subject to objective scientific analysis and laws; it behaves in a predictable manner. Marx was one of the first men to argue that economics could also be treated scientifically, that it also followed certain laws. He also contended that history followed certain patterns and that these patterns could be discovered and projected into the future. Marx did not claim that he could predict the future with certainty; he simply argued that, if conditions continued as they were at the present, certain things would probably happen in the future. If conditions changed, which they did (Marx had argued that they probably would not), the future would be different. Since they did change to some extent within his lifetime, some of Marx's positions changed, but he continued to believe that the basic projections he had made still held true. Finally, it must be noted that Marx believed that history was moving not only to a different stage but also to a better one. The pattern that he found in history and which he thought was a basic tool of analysis was the dialectic. Hegel, too, had argued that history was moving to different and better stages, and he also used the dialectic as his basic tool of analysis.

DIALECTICAL MATERIALISM

Probably the most difficult addition that Marx made to materialism was the dialectic. Therefore, his position is sometimes referred to as *dialectical materialism*. The dialectic seems to have originated in Greek thought as a means of attaining truth through a process of questions and answers. In answer to an original question, such as the meaning of courage, beauty, justice, or the like, a position is stated. The questioner then criticizes this position through the question and answer process until an opposite or significantly different position is taken. Then, by a continuation of the process, an attempt is made to arrive at the true parts of both positions. The process is then continued until all are satisfied that the correct answer has been

---

[12] The best statement of this position is still Friedrich Engels, *Socialism: Utopian and Scientific* (1880). Many editions are available.

reached. The most famous illustrations of this process can be found in the dialogues of Plato, such as the *Republic*.

Marx took the dialectic from Hegel, who argued that all ideas develop through this dialectical process of thesis (first position), antithesis (second position), and synthesis (truth of the opposites), which becomes a new thesis and thus continues the process. Figure 4–1 represents the most common and most

FIGURE 4–1
The dialectic

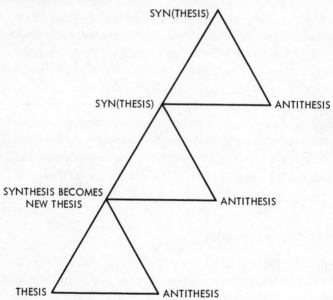

simple way of picturing the process. This illustration shows us something of what both Hegel and Marx are getting at. Starting at the bottom with the original thesis (first position), we see its "opposite" in the antithesis (second position). This opposition is not one of complete difference; it is produced from the thesis in one of two ways, spelled out in the first two laws of the dialectic.

1. *The transformation of quantity into quality.* Changes in degree gradually produce a change in quality or kind. The usual example is the change in water from a solid (ice), to a liquid, to a gas. The changes Hegel had in mind were more basic, say H_2O to H_2O_2.

2. *Unity or identity of opposites.* Contradictions in the thesis become the antithesis. (See change of quantity into quality.) Thus, the opposites are actually one. In addition, the thesis and antithesis become unified, differently, in the synthesis.

This unification of the thesis and the antithesis is produced through the third law of the dialectic:

3. *Negation of the negation.* Contradictions continue to accumulate until another qualitative change is made and the synthesis is reached. The synthesis, or the unity of the opposites, is a qualitative change as was the original step from the thesis to the antithesis. In other words, a new position is reached that is not simply the combination of the thesis and antithesis. In a similar way, chemists sometimes speak of synthesizing a new product from two or more products. Thus water, H_2O, is a synthesis of two parts hydrogen with one part oxygen to produce a product that is significantly different from the original components. The synthesis is then treated as a new product, and the process continues in the same manner. These three laws are often neglected or slighted by students of Marx, but, as will be seen later, they help to provide an understanding of the pattern taken by his analysis of history.[13]

It must be stressed that the general form of the dialectic is the interaction and intermingling of ideas, attitudes, beliefs, and positions, not the specific form used here as an example of the dialectic. A particularly relevant example would be on the order that none of the ideologies presented here are, by themselves, an accurate reflection of the world, but, on the other hand, each of them has something valuable to contribute to the understanding of how men behave. Ideological positions constantly interact in the world and are changed by that interaction. This very complex constant interaction and change give us a more comprehensive view of the dialectic.

----

[13] Marx did not attempt to apply the dialectic systematically to the material world. Some of his followers, such as Engels and Lenin, have tried to view nature as changing dialectically and have spoken vaguely of scientific laws operating dialectically, but almost without exception these attempts have been fruitless and irrelevant and need not be discussed here. The student who is interested in these attempts should consult the following works: Friedrich Engels, *Anti-Dühring: Herr Eugen Dühring's Revolution in Science,* Part 1, any edition; Friedrich Engels, *Dialectics of Nature,* any edition; and V. I. Lenin, *Materialism and Empirio-Criticism; Critical Comments on a Reactionary Philosophy,* chap. v, any edition.

HISTORICAL MATERIALISM

Marx applied the dialectic to his interpretation of history. Since any change in the economic system is gradually reflected in changes in the entire superstructure, Marx argued that it would be possible to interpret all of history from this perspective. He also contended that it might be possible to make some general statements about the future on the same basis. Again, it should be remembered that Marx did not say that he could predict the future. What he did say was that there were patterns in history that would in all probability continue into the future. Thus, an understanding of history should enable a scholar to argue that, if conditions remain the same, certain things were likely to take place in the future.

The major problem in discovering more precisely how Marx meant to explain all this is found in his use of economics, particularly the modes of production. Marx contended that economics is an exact science, but nowhere does he clearly define the nature of these modes of production, which are basic to an understanding of Marxian economics. It is possible to conclude that they consist of:

1. Available natural resources.
2. Productive techniques.
3. Organization of production (sometimes omitted).

But each of these components has certain potential problems which Marx did not always avoid. The first component is complicated by one of the most confusing points in Marxism, the role assigned to the human mind in the process of forming knowledge. Many natural resources are always readily available; but without the knowledge of how to use them, they are not, in fact, available. For example, uranium was not a useful natural resource until recently. Thus, it would seem that some knowledge must be gained before any natural resources are available to people. Marx does not deal with this point adequately, but in a sense he does not have to because it is clear that somehow or other human beings started using natural resources; it is only a relatively minor point in the philosophy to explain exactly how that took place. Still, it is unfortunate that Marx did not deal with the problem as it leaves a minor unexplained gap.

As humans gain in knowledge of the uses to which natural resources can be put, their mode of production changes, and they begin to develop tools and processes of manufacture. They begin to produce pottery or weave baskets; they learn to form metals into tools and weapons. These changes in turn lead to further changes in both the mode of production and the super-structure. The problem here in Marx's analysis is in large part due to our perception of the process as opposed to Marx's. We believe that such developments and changes must come about through the learning of certain techniques and then chang-ing them through a conscious search for better ways of doing things. In essence, we are seeing the situation from the view-point of the individual, whereas Marx is looking for a histori-cal process.

Certainly, it is possible to maintain that a historical process is merely the accumulation of changes wrought by individuals, but we should try to understand Marx's position before argu-ing with it. Here Marx is making a very simple point. He is say-ing that changes in productive techniques are brought about because previous changes were made. In other words, each development sets the stage for a further development. Finally, he is also saying that major changes in productive techniques, such as, for example, from herding to agriculture, produce major changes in the organization of the society involved and in the belief system of that society. In the case cited, he is ob-viously right. Although the change from herding to agriculture is an obvious case where major changes in productive tech-niques do change the organization of society, and specifically the political system of that society, Marx is probably correct in assuming that *any* such major change does produce a major change in the society. It is again obviously true that the change from a predominantly agricultural society to a predominantly industrial society has produced many far-reaching changes in contemporary society, and there are many who argue that sim-ilar far-reaching changes will occur as production becomes more and more highly automated.[14]

The third factor, organization of production, is the most complex because, if it refers to the organization of industry or

---

[14] See, for example, Herbert Marcuse, *An Essay on Liberation* (Boston: Bea-con Press, 1969).

the like, it must be viewed as part of the superstructure rather than of the modes of production. When Marx means simply the labor applied through tools to the natural resources, there is no problem. The problem is found in the phrase "the organization of production" because our contemporary connotations connected with the word *organization* imply a structure of some sort or a system of interrelated individuals that comprise a social unit. If this were true, this would clearly refer to part of the superstructure, but what Marx meant by the phrase, which kept it from being part of the superstructure, is contained in the word *production*. This implies that Marx is talking about labor and specifically about labor using tools to produce goods and not the method in which industry is organized.

Normally Marx is talking about labor when he speaks of the organization of production, but it can be said with equal confidence that sometimes he seems to mean something like the organization of industry. When he means the latter, he is obviously being inconsistent because the organization of industry is certainly one part of the superstructure.

Part of the superstructure produced by the modes of production is a set of *relations of production* or property relations. These constitute the second key to Marx's theory of history. Property relations in Marx's terminology refer to the ownership of the means of production, land, property, and so on. These property relations change more slowly than do the modes of production, and therefore a conflict is formed which can only be solved by a change in the property relations. This point is important for an understanding of Marx's analysis of the changes in history and for his criticism of contemporary society. Marx argued that property relations tend to evolve much more slowly than modes of production, and property relations will have a tendency not to change to meet changing needs. Since his analysis states that property relations are a product of the modes of production, it is clear that it is the property relations that must change to meet the new modes of production rather than the reverse. But, in the meantime, there is a tension between the modes of production and the property relations that is unresolved and cannot be resolved until the more slowly changing property relations have in fact changed.

This tension produces conflict within society and may in fact be one of the major reasons for the coming of a possible revolution and of Marx's certainty that the proletariat would win the revolution. He is saying that in a given case the owners of property will not be willing to give up their ownership, even though such a change is dictated by a change in the modes of production. At the same time, they ultimately must give up such property ownership because of the change in the modes of production. Thus, one can see in operation the three laws of the dialectic mentioned above. There is the transformation of quantity into quality in the changes in the modes of production. There is the unity of opposites in the growing contradiction between the economic foundation and the superstructure. And, finally, there is the negation of the negation in arriving at the new synthesis of modes of production and superstructure.

In addition, Marx uses the dialectic in his conception of the progression to higher and higher, or better and better, stages of society. This, in essence, is the idea of progress or the notion that man and society are inevitably moving to better things. An extremely popular idea in Marx's time, the idea of progress has fallen somewhat into disrepute today. Still Marx's use of the idea of progress is worthy of some further consideration.

Although it would not be appropriate to go into the complexities of the idea of progress, it should be understood that it was not simply the notion of the world getting better and better every day in every way. Of course, some believers in progress did think that the world was constantly getting better and that the human race had nothing to do with it. They argued that the world was moving in a straight line from some primitive state to some ultimate utopia or millennium in which everything would be good and beautiful. They believed that all people had to do was to wait and things would get better. But most of the believers in the idea of progress did not accept this simple formulation but developed a somewhat modified notion. It included the idea that the world, although improving, constantly fell away from the line of progress into some sort of corruption, and then only by great effort, perhaps a revolution, was the world able to be brought back onto the correct path.

This point raises a second consideration in the idea of progress; that is, that the path taken by the world in its gradual betterment could be affected both for good and evil by humanity. Marx seemed to have assumed, as did most of the other theorists of the idea of progress, that the world would gradually get better in spite of whatever human beings happened to do. But at the same time, he contended that people could improve themselves and the world as a whole through concerted action. Thus, humanity's position would improve, but knowledgeable people, such as Marx, were in a position to recognize the direction that must be taken in order to achieve this. The importance of this point in Marx will become apparent as we discuss Lenin's theory of the Communist party.

THE CLASS STRUGGLE

An important key to an understanding of Marxism is the concept of the *class struggle*. The class struggle is an hypothesis that Marx felt explained the period in which he lived. The class struggle is based on the contradiction between the modes of production and the relations of production just mentioned. It is this contradiction that produces the class struggle. Marx contended that in the mid-19th century the means of production were controlled by a class he called the *bourgeoisie*. This class did little if any work, but reaped immense profits from its control of the means of production. The actual labor was done by a class Marx called the *proletariat*. The mode of production required the proletariat, but it did not, according to Marx, require the bourgeoisie. Therefore, a struggle between these two classes results. Each wished to control the means of production. For Marx there was no question concerning the result—the proletariat was necessary, the bourgeoisie was not. Although he, and later Marxists, did attempt to apply the theory of the class struggle to all history, he argued that the best example of it existed in the mid-19th century in which society was clearly split into these two classes, the bourgeoisie or the capitalists, and the proletariat or the laboring class.

It is important at the outset to be clear regarding the nature of classes and of these two classes in particular. Classes are economic in nature and are groups of men ordered according to their relationship to the nonhuman powers of production and each other. The proletariat is the class that makes its living from the sale of its labor power. The bourgeoisie consists of the owners of the productive resources upon which the proletariat works. This class makes its living primarily from profit, interest, and rent, although it may earn some of its income from wages paid for managerial work and for the coordination of risk-taking ventures.

Many other smaller classes existed, but they were irrelevant to the unfolding conflict. In addition, Marx had a few problems with the manner in which he included certain groups within the class system. For example, he was always unclear as to exactly where the peasantry would fit within his system. He often included the peasantry in a group loosely known as the *petite bourgeoisie* because they were landowners. At other times he split his definition of the peasantry into a variety of groups ranging from the bourgeoisie to the proletariat, but he was never clear as to exactly where to place the group of peasantry who owned their land and worked it themselves. This problem of classification has plagued Marxist theorists ever since. No one is ever quite certain where to place the peasant. In addition to the peasantry, Marx also added another class at the bottom of his classification scheme called the *lumpenproletariat,* which was composed of the dregs of society, primarily thieves, bums, and the like. Marx never clarified whether it would be possible ever to include this group within the proletariat itself, but one would assume from his writings that he did think that at some point after the revolution it would be possible to incorporate the *lumpenproletariat* into the proletariat in the same way that the bourgeoisie was to be incorporated.[15] It should be kept in mind, though, that for Marx the most important classes were the proletariat and the bourgeoisie.

The class struggle can be seen through the three laws of the dialectic. The development of industrialization produced the bourgeoisie and proletariat. These classes, although originally

---

[15] For discussion of these problems, see John Plamenatz, *Man and Society: A Critical Examination of Some Important Social and Political Theories from Machiavelli to Marx* (London: Longmans Green & Co., 1963), vol. 2, pp. 293–300, and David Mitrany, *Marx against the Peasant: A Study in Social Dogmatism* (New York: Collier Books, 1961).

unified because they were for a time both necessary for the development of industrialization, become more antagonistic until they become thesis and antithesis. This is partially the effect of the growing wealth of the bourgeoisie combined with the growing poverty of the proletariat and partially the effect of the gradual failure of capitalism. Thus, we have the transformation of quantity into quality and the unity of opposites. The split gradually widens until it becomes intolerable, and we reach the negation of the negation, which produces a social revolution, and the synthesis is reached. This dialectical change must, of course, be seen as part of the broader conflict between modes of production and the property relations through which they are experienced.

REVOLUTION[16]

A revolution was supposed to develop as a result of the series of crises that capitalism was to experience. They failed to appear as regularly or as seriously as Marx had expected, and thus the revolution did not develop, or, as a contemporary Marxist would put it, has not yet developed as he had anticipated. In a small book entitled, *Imperialism; the Highest Stage of Capitalism,* Lenin attempted to show why these crises failed to occur as predicted. He argued that by colonizing and exploiting underdeveloped countries, the capitalists were temporarily able to stave off these crises. Colonial exploitation made it possible to pay the workers slightly better by providing the capitalists with:

1.   Cheap raw materials.
2.   Cheap labor.
3.   Markets for manufactured goods and excess capital.

He believed that imperialism merely postponed the revolution; it did not put it off permanently. It lulls the proletariat into believing that revolution will not be necessary.[17] Therefore,

---

[16] Here we leave Marx temporarily and turn to his followers.

[17] Alfred G. Meyer provides an excellent analysis of Lenin's theory of imperialism and its implications. See Alfred G. Meyer, *Leninism* (New York: Frederick A. Praeger, 1962), chaps. xi and xii. See also the discussion of neocolonialism in Chapter 8 of this book.

Lenin and Mao Tse-tung developed means for fomenting and directing a successful revolution.

In discussing the Marxian approach to revolution, it is instructive to distinguish between two different types of revolution—the political and the social. The political revolution takes place when political power is seized by the proletariat. The social revolution takes place later, first, through changes made in the property relations of society and, second, as the superstructure adjusts to these changes.

Marx usually saw the political revolution as violent, although he did allow for the possibility of peaceful change. The revolution would probably be violent for two reasons. First, Marx argued that achieving the synthesis would always be sudden; thus the gradualness implicit in peaceful change was ruled out by the dialectic. Second, the bourgeoisie would never agree to its disappearance as a class and would force the proletariat into a violent revolution. In addition, Marx believed that revolution was good and necessary and worked for it himself.

Lenin's contribution was the development of the revolutionary party, which was an organizational weapon in the struggle to overthrow capitalism. Lenin argued that such a party was necessary because the proletariat was incapable of recognizing its role as the revolutionary class whereas the party provided this necessary consciousness. As Alfred G. Meyer has stated, "The party is conceived as the organization, incarnation, or institutionalization of class consciousness."[18] The party would be made up of those who had achieved this consciousness and had also become professional revolutionists. In the popular phrase, the party was to be the "vanguard of the proletariat"; it would point the way and lead the proletariat to its goal.

The party was to be the mechanism for spurring man on to the higher stage of progress that we mentioned earlier in discussing the dialectic as an expression of the idea of progress. Since the idea of progress includes the possibility of an individual, a group, or some institution helping to move the world on to a higher plane, it is clear that within Communist ideology, this role was to be fulfilled by the party. The party, "the vanguard of the proletariat," was to be the instrument that

---

[18] Ibid., pp. 32–33.

would be used to ensure continued progress. It would bring together the divided masses of workers, and it would express what they were truly feeling but were incapable of expressing. It would mold, unify, and make them into a force for a change to something better. They would be the vehicle to overcome the conservatism of the property owners who had become outmoded, and they would, perhaps through a revolution, remove the property from the hands of its current owners and redistribute it through the mechanism of the party.

It should be kept in mind that the proletarians as individual members of a class would not be likely to recognize their historic role. In the first place, they would be much too busy attempting to stay alive to be concerned with class questions. Second, very few would ever identify themselves as class members. Thus, it would be left up to the few who become aware, the party members, to prepare for the great role the proletariat would play.

The importance of Lenin's party is found in the idea of the professional revolutionary and in the organizational principle, democratic centralism. Although the party would be composed of a small conspiratorial group of professional revolutionists, Lenin believed that it should develop contacts throughout the society as a whole, since no revolution could be successful without the support of, or at least little direct opposition from, the largest part of the population of the country. This meant that the party members would have to have a variety of organizational skills. They would have to be experts at agitation and propaganda. Since they had to be able to establish and maintain a vast network of "front" organizations throughout the country, they would have to be expert administrators. Ideally, prior to the revolution, the majority of the population should be organized into a variety of these groups which would also provide the basis for organization once the revolution has succeeded. (Figure 4–2 illustrates the party's position.) In addition, the party member would have to constantly prepare for the revolution, since it would come only when the masses suddenly revolted against their oppressors.

Ideally, the party might light the spark[19] that set the masses

---

[19] The theory of the spark is important for Lenin. One of his newspapers was called The Spark (Iskra), and he often refers to the necessity of some incident igniting the masses.

FIGURE 4–2
The Communist party and the society

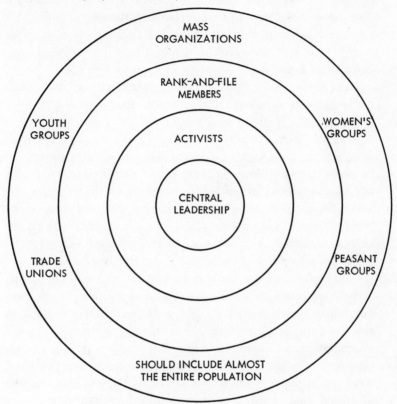

afire, but the spark might come anywhere, anytime, and the party had to be in readiness to ride the revolution into power. Clearly, Lenin believed that it was possible for the party to produce the necessary conditions for a revolution, but it is equally certain that he believed that it was impossible to be absolutely sure when the revolution would come. Hence, the party must always be prepared for the revolution coming at an unexpected, perhaps even an unpropitious, time.

The principle of organization that would make all this possible is democratic centralism. This principle combines freedom of discussion with centralized control and responsibility. Before any decision is made by the party, there should be complete freedom to dissent; after the decision is made, it must be accepted unanimously. Lenin felt that this principle could function adequately, since the party members started from a position of agreement regarding goals. In practice, freedom of discussion was often forgotten. Democratic centralism would also serve as the principle of organization in the period immediately following the revolution, which will be discussed more completely later.

As a technique of revolutionary organization, democratic centralism has important characteristics that must not be overlooked. If one is planning a revolution, care must be taken to organize one's followers in such a way that they can be brought into action at a moment's notice. They must also be able to be brought into action in a completely concerted manner without disagreements or squabbles over what is to be done now and what is to be done later, or arguments about the correct techniques of taking over the government, or who is to do this or that at a particular moment. It is absolutely essential that there be complete agreement among the revolutionists over the techniques of the revolution and the organization of society immediately after the successful revolution. Democratic centralism provides this by giving the leaders complete control over the actions of the revolutionists while at the same time allowing all members of the party to participate freely and openly in the process of reaching the appropriate decisions. Again, it should be noted that democratic centralism has usually been used in ways that have stressed centralism.

Other Marxist theorists have also contributed to the techniques of revolution. For example, Mao Tse-tung's theory of guerrilla warfare is also an organizational weapon. Mao's theory can be divided into two parts, the strictly military principles and some political principles that are derived from one of the military principles. The military principles are as follows:

1. Attack dispersed, isolated enemy forces first; attack concentrated strong enemy forces later.
2. Take small and medium cities and extensive rural areas first; take big cities later.
3. Make the wiping out of the enemy's effective strength our main objective; do not make holding or seizing a city or place our main objective.
4. In every battle to concentrate an absolutely superior force . . . to encircle the enemy forces completely, strive to wipe them out thoroughly and do not let any escape from the net.

5. Fight no battle unprepared, fight no battle if we are not sure of winning. . . .
6. Give full play to our style of fighting—courage in battle, no fear of sacrifice, no fear of fatigue, and continuous fighting (that is, fighting successive battles in a short time without rest).
7. Strive to wipe out the enemy through mobile warfare. At the same time, pay attention to the tactics of positional attack and capture enemy fortified points and cities.
8. With regard to attacking cities, resolutely seize all enemy fortified points and cities which are weakly defended.
9. Replenish our strength with all the arms and most of the personnel captured from the enemy.
10. Make good use of the intervals between campaigns to rest, train, and consolidate our troops.[20]

This last point requires a territorial base where the guerrillas will be virtually free from attack so that they will be able to rest, train, and so on. In order to achieve this, they must have the positive support of the people in that area. This support is gained by: (1) establishing a peasant government; (2) allowing the peasants to redistribute the land; and (3) helping the peasants in whatever rebuilding activities they undertake. The territorial base will thus provide food, manpower, and, perhaps most importantly, experience in organization. The network of tunnels used by the Viet Cong during the Vietnam war provided a similar resting place. Thus, Mao's theory of guerrilla warfare fulfills basically the same function as Lenin's theory of the revolutionary party. Mao's approach to revolution is of growing importance today and, therefore, it is important to recognize that the tactics outlined above are designed with the same purposes in mind as were Lenin's strategies.

The theory of the revolution is primarily concerned with tactics, not philosophy, although many of the purely tactical questions are important for understanding the underlying theory. Probably the most outstanding issue is the one of violence versus nonviolence. Historically, violence has been virtually the sole answer, even though Marx had argued that it might not be essential. More recently, the whole point of revolution

---

[20] Mao Tse-tung, *Selected Works* (Peking: Foreign Language Press, 1961), vol. 4, pp. 161–62. Only the main points have been stated. Mao qualified his arguments with comments on tactics for the later period when the guerrilla force has gained greatly in strength.

has been toned down by many, but not all, Marxist theorists. Contemporary Marxist theorists of the more conservative approach argue that violent revolution may not be necessary or desirable except, perhaps, in the developing countries, and even there it may not be required. This argument rests on a number of assumptions:

1. Revolution may not be possible in most developed countries.
2. The developing countries may be more easily convinced by examples of rapid economic growth than by violence.
3. Revolutionary forms may not be readily exportable.[21]
4. Contemporary revolutions are often more nearly nationalist than Communist.

For all these reasons the tactics are changing. The extremist Marxists, often followers of Mao Tse-tung, or, more recently, Leon Trotsky (real name: Lev Davidovich Bronstein 1877–1940),[22] are not convinced. They contend that the rejection of revolution is a rejection of Marx and Engels and cannot be accepted. They are often particularly concerned with the developing countries, or use examples from these countries, and contend that the leaders of these countries, although not usually traditional capitalists, must be replaced by Communists. Although this may not require a revolution, it is likely that this will be the only way the proletariat will be able to gain power.

One of the peculiarities of the developing nations that causes problems for the Marxist theorist is the lack of a proletariat. This was first faced by Lenin in Russia. It was true in China at the time of the Communist revolution, and Mao attempted to base his revolutionary techniques on the peasants as a revolutionary class rather than the proletariat. Nevertheless, it is usually argued that the proletariat is the most revolutionary class, even in the developing countries where the proletariat is either nonexistent or exists only in very small numbers. And if a revo-

---

[21] See Regis Debray, *Revolution in the Revolution? Armed Struggle and Political Struggle in Latin America*, trans. Bobbye Oritz (New York: Monthly Review Press, 1967). See also Regis Debray, *Strategy for Revolution*, ed. Robin Blackburn (New York: Monthly Review Press, 1970), and *Prison Writings*, trans. Rosemary Sheed (London: A. Lane, 1973).

[22] Trotsky's ideas will be discussed in Chapter 7.

lution is successful without a proletariat, as it was in China, much effort is put into developing a proletarian class immediately after the revolution. This, of course, is necessary anywhere in the modern world because, without a large laboring class, industrialization is impossible. Therefore, a dictatorship of the proletariat is introduced, even where the proletariat is virtually nonexistent.

This problem of the lack of the proletariat in many developing nations, or at least of a proletariat in the industrial sense as Marx usually used the term, does cause serious problems for the Marxist theorist who is attempting to discuss the developing nations. The problem is not so much in the period of the revolution, although supposedly the proletariat should lead the revolution. It is partially a theoretical, and partially a practical, problem after the revolution. The developing nations, without exception, wish to industrialize. They cannot, in fact, industrialize without the development of an industrial proletariat. Therefore, for the theoretical reasons of the Marxian ideology which requires a proletariat, and the very practical reason of the desire and need for industrialization, one of the first steps that any Marxist leader in a developing country takes is to develop or attempt to develop a proletariat.

DICTATORSHIP OF THE PROLETARIAT

After the revolution, Marx envisioned a brief transitional period known as the dictatorship of the proletariat. This stage was to be characterized by the consolidation of the power of the proletariat through the gradual disappearance of the bourgeoisie and the minor classes as they became part of the proletariat. Marx did not envision the physical destruction of the bourgeoisie and the minor classes that took place in the Soviet Union primarily under Stalin. Marx viewed the dictatorship of the proletariat as a period in which these classes would be incorporated into the proletariat by making them laborers, not by destroying them. In other words, the bourgeoisie and the other classes would be given jobs that would, over time, change their outlook on life and make them good members of the proletariat. This would be the period in which the entire superstructure would slowly change to adjust to the socialist mode of production. Loosely, the dictatorship of the proletariat should have the following characteristics:

1. Distribution of income according to labor performed.
2. Gradual disappearance of classes.
3. The state in the hands of the proletariat.
4. Increasing productivity.
5. Increasing socialist consciousness—people work with few incentives.
6. Increasing equality.
7. A command economy.
8. The economy managed by the state.

All of these characteristics were supposed to be changing fairly rapidly and the dictatorship of the proletariat was to be brief. In practice, no country that has followed Marx's ideas has yet moved beyond the dictatorship of the proletariat. A number of countries in the world today are in what they call the dictatorship of the proletariat. Contrary to Marx, this "transitional" period does not seem to focus on the economic system. One could almost say that the dictatorship of the proletariat as practiced is based on the political system with all else as superstructure rather than being based on the economic system.[23]

Within the political system, the central position is held by the Communist party. This is true for two reasons, both of which derive from Lenin. First, the Communist party is defined as the vanguard of the proletariat, and in any state governed by the proletariat it should automatically rule. Second, Lenin and the Communist party successfully took power in the first Communist revolution and established all of the machinery of government. Thus, the Communist party formed the government and might be expected to run it. (Figure 4–3 illustrates the typical organization of a Communist party.)

The major function of any political system is to integrate or pull together the society into one functioning unit and to maintain order. For these purposes, it is given broad coercive powers to help ensure that its orders are carried out. The Communist party does not technically hold these powers itself, but in

---

[23] At this point we turn to a consideration of some aspects of current Communist practice and leave the theory temporarily.

FIGURE 4–3
Organization of a Communist party

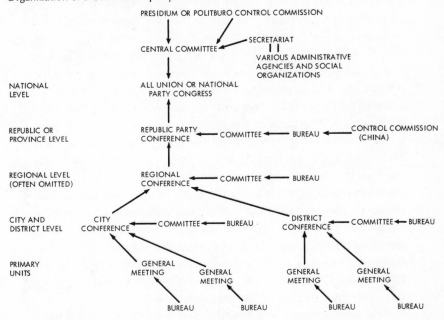

effect it acts as the government in most cases. In so acting, it requires an organization that has contacts throughout the entire society. In many ways, this is a carry-over of Lenin's theory of a party which would ideally touch upon the great mass of the people, or the entire people, through a wide variety of mass organizations, each organized on the same basis and each intimately connected with the party. The principle of organization, which has been mentioned above, is *democratic centralism*. In operation, democratic centralism acts to provide channels of information for the leadership and as a means of relaying directions throughout the country and ensuring that the directions are followed. It should also be recalled that Lenin's theory of the party included the idea that the top leadership in the party should be skilled administrators and organizers. Thus, it should not be at all surprising that many of the leaders of the party hold comparable positions in the state administration.

One final point needs to be made about the party. The party is not as simple as the organizational chart implies. Although the centralist side of democratic centralism is stressed, there are many different individuals with varying points of view and programs competing for the ear of the top leadership. Hence, in practice, the party is made up of many competing groups. For example, there may be a group arguing that more money should be put into agriculture, another pushing light industry, a third the space program. There may be a group that wants a buildup of the military and another that wants the military de-emphasized. The party is the major avenue for the expression of these competing viewpoints. In addition, demands are made upon the party leadership from elements outside the party such as the military or the educational system. Although the ultimate decision is made by the party leadership, the various demands must be carefully sorted out and assigned priorities. None can be completely neglected for long, or a section of the society and probably a section of the party itself will be-come disillusioned with the leadership. Thus, the party appears to be monolithic, but this is only partially correct and is a much too simplified picture of its operation.

One of the major concerns that has split the party has been economic planning, which is the core of the economic system. As would be expected, the party plays the determining role in establishing the economic goals and priorities. Without going into great detail about the process or the administrative orga-nizations involved, the economic system operates as follows. Detailed data is collected from throughout the country regard-ing the available resources and productive capacity and the minimum needs of each area of the economy. Political deci-sions are made determining what to produce. This is the key decision. It is only possible to produce so much within a given period, and this means that, if the greatest emphasis is placed on consumer goods, heavy industry may have to be slighted. Some sort of balance must be reached that will fulfill the mini-mum needs in each area. Beyond this essential minimum the party decides what part or parts of the economy will be stressed, and the planners allocate the raw materials and set quotas ac-cordingly. This is the meaning of a command economy man-aged by the state. Each industry, each agricultural section, is told what to produce and in what amounts.

A command economy means that the distribution of agricultural and manufactured goods is centrally controlled. Usually there is some flexibility in this, and there are often open markets where some agricultural goods and craft work is sold. The distribution of income is also controlled by the state, and, in the period of the dictatorship of the proletariat, this is done according to work performed so that there is room for flexibility here, too, and there is no attempt at any leveling of income.[24]

China has made a change in this system that has far-reaching implications for the entire social system. This is the *commune system*. Basically, the commune system is a means of economic organization for the most efficient use of manpower, but it also is a means of political control and, the Chinese say, a step beyond the dictatorship of the proletariat. A rural commune is formed by abandoning a few villages in an area and bringing the people together into one large village. Thus, because they are not so spread out, the people are easier to control, and there is a fairly large pool of labor that can be readily shifted from agriculture to road building to dike repair as the seasons change and the need arises. The urban commune is organized in a similar manner by taking all the workers from a particular factory or industry.

The commune is not merely an economic organization. It is a miniature state even though it is not self-governing. At the beginning, men, women, and children were separated in an attempt to break up the old family system, but this was rapidly changed and the nuclear family of husband and wife, children, and possibly grandparents is the basis of the commune. During the day the children are either cared for by the older women in nurseries or go to school. Other women prepare food for the entire commune, and common dining halls are the rule. Thus, many women are freed from child care and household duties to join the men in the fields or in some other work. The Chinese claim that the commune system is the basis for the new society to come after the dictatorship of the proletariat, and therefore they spend a great deal of time and effort in educating the members of the communes and the rest of

---

[24] All this is being reconsidered. Some thinkers are suggesting a regulated market system. See, for example, Wlodzimierz Brus, *The Economics and Politics of Socialism* (London: Routledge and Kegan Paul, 1974).

the population in the great advantages that supposedly come with commune life.[25]

According to Marx, the dictatorship of the proletariat is a period of transition from the old, bad society to a new, good one. Previously, we have briefly glanced at Marx's picture of society under capitalism. Now, let us see to what extent the dictatorship of the proletariat has corrected the evils that Marx saw in capitalist society. In the first place, religion is disappearing. In the Soviet Union, religion is strongly discouraged but tolerated and is fairly free except that it cannot run schools. There is widespread discrimination against Jews. In China, there has never been a great emphasis on religion, but the old philosophical and ethical systems, such as Confucianism and Taoism and the fairly small religious groups are being abolished. The family is much the same as described in the Chinese commune, except that outside of the commune, women are not free from housework. In all Communist countries there are state-run nurseries which free women from child care, and there is a great concern with the entire socialization system.

This is illustrated by the fact that the major change under the dictatorship of the proletariat has been in education. From earliest childhood in the nurseries through widespread adult education, there is a concentrated effort to raise the educational level of the entire population while at the same time teaching the values of the new social system. In undertaking this immense task, all the available means of mass communication are being used in addition to the more traditional classroom techniques. In China, in particular, the individual is constantly surrounded by propaganda broadcast over loudspeakers on the corner, in trains, in the factories, and in the fields.

In addition, most individuals are members of one or more of the mass organizations, such as labor unions or youth groups. This is a carry-over from the system of democratic centralism and the stress on involving the entire society in the revolution through a wide variety of mass organizations. These groups are comparable to the same sort of informal or formal private or-

[25] An excellent picture of a Chinese commune can be found in Jack Chen, *A Year in Upper Felicity; Life in a Chinese Village during the Cultural Revolution* (New York: Macmillan Co., 1973).

ganizations that exist in the United States and other countries—
the various fraternal organizations; organizations such as the
Boy Scouts, the Girl Scouts, Campfire Girls, and so forth; and
the various professional organizations, such as the American
Medical Association and the American Bar Association. These
organizations in the Communist countries are quasi-official and
are intended to help inculcate the values of the system. In the
United States, these organizations clearly serve the same purpose, but they do not have a clear official status.

The entire educational system is consciously designed to impart the values of the system in addition to providing the individual with the training necessary for him to take his place
as a useful member of society. Again, the differences between
this type of educational system and the type of educational
system that is found in the United States, for example, is that
there is a clear-cut, conscious effort to impart the values of
the system to the individual. The system in the United States
does the same thing, but it is not as clearly organized for that
purpose. From the earliest grades we teach the children patriotic little stories about the founding fathers, such as George
Washington and the cherry tree, that are intended to present
certain values to the child and at the same time present a good
image of the American government. The fact that many of these
stories are untrue and are therefore, in this particular example,
directly opposed to what the story is trying to teach does not
seem to bother anybody.

We teach other stories, such as the tale about "the little
train that could." We tell children that if they try hard enough,
they can do anything. We know that this is not quite true, but
we tell the story anyway. Another example is the story of the
little train that left the tracks and got into all sorts of trouble.
When he got back onto the tracks, he was happy, contented,
and accepted; the story is obviously suggesting that conformity is good. It is also obviously indicating that acceptance by
the group is a goal to be strived for, which is, of course, just
another way of looking at the conformity question.[26] As can be

---

[26] For a discussion of this type of story, see David Riesman, *The Lonely Crowd: A Study of the Changing American Character* (Garden City, N.Y.: An-chor Books, 1953), pp. 128–31.

seen, our educational system is doing exactly the same thing as the educational system in any other country. This is one of the things that any educational system is designed to do. The values that are taught vary considerably from country to country, and, of course, one of the purposes of this book is to look at those values that are taught in various countries.

The key difference in the approaches to socialization in many countries is the degree to which there is a conscious attempt to direct the values of the future generations. We know that in the Soviet Union and in China there is a clear, thoroughgoing attempt to do this. We also know that in countries such as the United States and England there is also an attempt to do this. But it is not as clearly defined or as consciously recognized, and, because of this, it is impossible for there to be a truly concerted effort to direct values. The lack of such a concerted effort plus the essentially pluralistic character of the country means that there will be nowhere near the same degree of success or even of effort.

One final segment of the social system remains to be mentioned, the social stratification system. There is considerable misunderstanding of what Marxism and communism have to say regarding social stratification. Engels said that "the proletarian demand for equality is the demand for *abolition of classes*. Any demand for equality which goes beyond that, of necessity passes into absurdity."[27] Thus, Marxism did not argue for the complete elimination of stratification. And communism has certainly not eliminated it. Both stratification and mobility seem to depend on two factors, membership in the party and education, particularly scientific and technical education. At the same time, an effort is made to achieve some degree of social equality. Concerts, the theater, and all cultural and recreational facilities are made equally available to all, and in this way some of the edge is taken off the stratification system.

FULL COMMUNISM

The changes in contemporary communism brought about by the fusion of nationalism, the early writings of Marx, and exis-

---

[27] Engels, *Anti-Dühring*, pp. 147–48. Emphasis in the original.

tentialism have given rise to a resurgence of utopian thinking by Marxists. But they have not significantly changed the characteristics of Marx's ideal system, Full or Pure Communism. Full Communism has the following characteristics:

1. Distribution of income according to need, no longer according to labor performed.
2. No classes.
3. The state withers away.
4. Very high productivity, so that there is plenty for all.
5. High socialist consciousness—people work without incentives.
6. More equality but not absolute equality.
7. No money.
8. A command economy.
9. The economy managed by a free and equal association of producers.
10. The differences between occupations disappear, so that there is no social distinction between town and country.
11. Each person does about as much physical as intellectual labor.
12. The system, as Stalin was the first to show, is worldwide.[28]

Full Communism is the goal of the entire system, the utopia toward which all else is aimed. Its general characteristics are not much different from the utopias created by a variety of other socialists throughout the centuries, but some of these characteristics are worth further mention.

The economic aspects of Full Communism are outlined above, and the major similarities and differences between it and the dictatorship of the proletariat are illustrated. The command economy still exists, but it is no longer controlled by the state. Marx was primarily concerned with abolishing exploitation, and in Full Communism there are no exploiters, only workers. With the exploiters totally gone and the people working without incentives, there should be plenty so that all can be rewarded according to need. The actual organization of the economic system poses a number of problems that will be discussed later.

---

[28] Adapted slightly and reprinted by permission of the author and the publishers from P. J. D. Wiles, *The Political Economy of Communism* (Cambridge, Mass.: Harvard University Press ©, 1962, by Basil Blackwell & Mott Ltd.), pp. 332–33. See also, Howard J. Sherman, "The Economics of Pure Communism," *Soviet Studies*, vol. 22 (July 1970), pp. 24–36.

When turning to other aspects of the society, it is obvious that the most direct effect of a change to Full Communism would be on the social stratification and mobility systems. Since classes would no longer exist and since no distinction would be made between types of labor, there should be little clear social stratification. In the classless or single-class society, there would be no basis for any significant distinctions among people. "Significant" for Marx meant economic, and it would be foolish to assume that he foresaw a complete leveling. Individual differences would remain, but they would no longer be distinctions that were detrimental to the individual or the society as they had been under capitalism and all the other socio-economic systems that preceded it. Occupational mobility would be increased greatly, since an individual would be able to move freely among those positions that interested him.

Marx envisioned other significant changes in the social system. There would, of course, be no religious system. There would be education for all. All crime would disappear because there would be no reason to react against society. In addition, he believed that with the coming of Full Communism prostitution and adultery would disappear and the monogamous family would become a reality. The new family would be based on a love-sex relationship that Marx believed could only have one focus. At the same time, he desired to free women to work. A contemporary Soviet scholar has suggested that under Full Communism there will be a change from personal housekeeping functions, such as cooking and cleaning, to public or communal services, thus freeing more women to enter the job market.[29]

With the coming of the classless society, the state would no longer be necessary and would disappear. But it would be replaced by "the administration of things," which means that the economic system would have to be organized and somebody would have to administer it. It would be administered by "a free and equal association of producers," which would have the authority to direct what should be produced and in

---

[29] E. G. Balagushkin, "The Building of Communism and the Evolution of Family and Marital Relations," *Soviet Sociology*, vol. 1 (Winter 1962/63), p. 43. Originally published in 1962 in *Voprosy Filosofii*.

what amounts, and how it should be distributed. This "free and equal association of producers" could conceivably take a wide variety of forms, depending upon the size of the territory and the complexity of industries within the territory. In attempting to reduce Marx's notion to its fundamentals, most such associations would undoubtedly follow some such pattern as follows. A committee would be selected, probably by election, that would collect data on the productive capacity of the region and the needs of the people. It would then establish priorities and goals for the various manufacturing plants, farms, and craft industries. This all assumes an economy based on abundance and thus would be more concerned with collecting accurate data on needs than establishing priorities. It would be a continuous process, and certainly the composition of the committee would change periodically. Thus, the committee would hold no coercive power, still assuming abundance, and would merely administer the economy.

Full Communism is obviously a utopia. It probably will not, even cannot, ever exist. But it is the goal of Marxism. Many Communists today believe that it will never come. Others believe that it is still possible. But, whichever position one takes, it illustrates some of the appeal that communism has had and will continue to have in the future.

CONTEMPORARY TRENDS

There are a number of recent developments in communism that need to be noted, including the influence of nationalism, trends in a number of Communist countries, and the attempt at a Marxist-Christian dialogue. Marx had believed that ultimately the world would all become Communist, both because this would be the best system and because the logic of the dialectic led in that direction. In assuming a worldwide communism, Marx had thought that class similarities would overcome national differences. This has not proven to be the case. From the very beginning, Communist parties in different countries argued that the revolution in their country would take place slower or faster than in other countries because of national differences. Even Marx had made this point, arguing that certain countries were ripe for revolution while others were not. Stalin also spoke of the development of "socialism in one country," meaning the USSR, and clearly expressed strongly nationalistic feelings. But this issue was not considered to be important because no one thought that the proletariat would put national sentiment before class sentiment. The fact that they did was seen in World War I and even before, since the proletariat flocked to the cause of the nation against the advice of Communist leaders.

The contemporary influence of nationalism on communism was begun by Marshal Tito of Yugoslavia, who early refused to follow the dictates of the Soviet Union under Stalin, the self-styled and, for a long time, the actual spokesman for communism as a whole. Since Stalin died in 1953, every Eastern European country has changed the nature of its relationship with the USSR. With the exception of Albania, which has formed a coalition of sorts with China, they still maintain close relations with the USSR and are clearly still in a subordinate position.

The reasons for these changes are complex, and we do not as yet have sufficient data for valid generalizations, but it seems clear that one of the more important reasons is nationalism. The peoples of these countries, while mostly viewing themselves as Communists, identify more closely with their nation than with communism or the Soviet Union. Each country has a distinct, individual history and culture that the people believe should not be submerged by communism.

A second aspect of contemporary communism which has already been mentioned—the split over the importance of revolution—reflects nationalism. Coexistence or detente with non-Communist countries has been the key to this difference. The moderates argue that coexistence is possible or even, because of the hydrogen bomb held by both sides, essential. Coexistence refers, according to Khrushchev,[30] to the different systems of government. It does not refer to different ideologies because communism is capable of demonstrating that it is a better system and hence will win out in the end through conversion or internal revolt by the proletariat—this was the mean-

---

[30] See Strobe Talbott, ed. and trans., *Khrushchev Remembers* (Boston: Little, Brown & Co., 1970), p. 512.

ing of Khrushchev's famous statement, "We will bury you."[31] The militants contend that this soft line merely puts off the inevitable conflict and is actually giving in to capitalism. This whole split is also part of a general shift away from radicalism on the part of successful revolutionary movements. However, this topic is beyond the scope of this book.

A third aspect of contemporary communism relates to the problem of leadership change, which is a particularly difficult problem for a dictatorial system. No Communist country has as yet developed a means of smoothly changing from one leader or dictator to the next. Thus, there is a constant struggle for power among the major potential dictators within each Communist country. This struggle for power has a tremendous influence on the way the system operates. It is impossible for any leader to be completely sure of the loyalty of his followers, and particularly, as the leader ages, there is a jockeying for position among his followers to see who takes over when he dies. Although it may seem that there is a high degree of unity, beneath the surface there is a constant turmoil. This has been clearly seen in the Soviet Union with the ouster of Khrushchev and the sparring among potential leaders since then. Contemporary communism in the period of the dictatorship of the proletariat has failed to provide the smooth transition that Marx had envisioned and has instead produced a system that seems to be incapable of smooth change.

Many Communist countries are currently in considerable turmoil, either because, as in the USSR and much of Eastern Europe, many people are trying to push the regime to allow greater individual freedom, or because, as in China, the regime is trying to keep up the revolutionary fervor of the people. In addition, countries such as Cuba and Yugoslavia are continuing their experiments in forms of worker's control, with varying degrees of success.

The problems in the Soviet Union due to the treatment of dissident writers and Jews who wish to emigrate to Israel has

---

[31] In his recent memoirs, Khrushchev reiterated this point saying that he meant that the proletariat in the United States would inevitably overthrow or bury the bourgeoisie. Ibid.

regularly made headlines in the Western world. These issues illustrate the difficulty that any authoritarian regime, not just Communist ones, seem to have with dissidence. Leaders in an authoritarian regime seem to believe that all dissent, reformist or revolutionist, attacks the very roots of the regime. This problem may also reflect the idea of democratic centralism—a decision, once made, is not to be questioned. Whatever the causes, this confrontation can be expected to continue, and it will be interesting to see if an authoritarian regime can adapt to internal dissent.

China illustrates another interesting problem, a regime that keeps its people in ferment and tries to keep the revolution alive. In so doing China has, particularly in the years of the cultural revolution (about 1966–69), attempted to change the basic pattern of Chinese life in many ways, and the results are just beginning to be assessed. Here we can only look briefly at a few examples. First, as was mentioned above, is the continued development of the commune system. These communes have been subdivided into smaller units for most matters, because they are generally too large to actively involve the entire population in the decision making of the commune. This involvement seems to be of two kinds. On the one hand, there appears to be a serious effort to give the community some actual authority to make decisions on a wide range of local matters. On the other hand, participation allows the leadership to direct, educate, and correct the masses by ensuring that the correct line is heard and understood by all. A second example of the nature of contemporary Chinese society might be the system of criticism. An individual who acts or speaks contrary to the established range of accepted behavior is likely to be subjected to a criticism session in which neighbors will point out his or her faults. A final related point is that a candidate for higher education must be elected by his or her workmates in the commune or factory. There is no possibility of going directly to college from secondary school. One works first, is chosen by one's workmates, and one also works at some agricultural or industrial job while in college.

There have also been continued attempts to change the nature of the Chinese family; attempts that have still met with only limited success. Many, if not most, marriages are still arranged, and the family is still the central focus of Chinese life. There has been considerable success in freeing women from their traditional role as servants to their fathers or husbands, but much of the traditional system remains.

Economically China and the commune system has been quite successful, particularly in agriculture. Politically, it is impossible to see where China is going, but the Chinese leaders, and a significant section of the population, take communism seriously and believe that they are on their way to building a truly Communist society.

Cuba and Yugoslavia are both attempting to build a more open Communist economy. Both are experimenting with far-reaching decentralization of the economy with the authority for decision making at the factory level with the workers making many of the basic decisions.[32] As part of this, there is in a number of Communist countries an attempt being made to introduce some aspects of the free market by providing a wider range of consumer goods with various models rather than just one.

The most important development for the basic theory of communism is found in the theories of self-management found predominantly in Yugoslavia. Many of the theorists of self-management have been treated as subversive in Yugoslavia and have lost their positions, but the theory is still being developed. Self-management includes the ideas of decentralization and workers control, but it does not take these ideas as far as some anarchists (see Chapter 6) would want. Under self-management national governmental apparatus will continue, but it will be nonauthoritarian and will encourage the development of free speech and a free press. Basically, self-management calls for the democratization of the entire social, economic, and political system. It does not mean the establishment of capitalism or the forms of government and society found in the West.[33]

A final contemporary trend, albeit one with about a ten-year history, is the Marxist-Christian dialogue. The modern dialogue

---

[32] Other aspects of worker's control will be discussed in Chapter 7.

[33] The best summary is found in Mihailo Marković, "Philosophical Foundations of Economic and Political Self-management," in Ted Honderich, ed., *Social Ends and Political Means* (London: Routledge & Kegan Paul, 1976), pp. 145–66.

began in 1965 with the publication of *From Anathema to Dialogue; The Challenge of Marxist-Christian Cooperation* by the French Marxist Roger Garaudy. Since then a large and growing literature has developed regarding the degree to which Marxist and Christian attitudes and insights are compatible. Although it is impossible to discuss this dialogue in detail, we can suggest some of the issues involved. The writings of the young Marx, focusing as they do on human alienation and Marx's critique of the dehumanizing effects of capitalist society, have attracted theologians who have had similar concerns. Some Marxists have found in Christianity, particularly early Christianity, a deep concern with the oppressed of the world and a message of hope for the future in this life. Therefore, both have begun to consider what they can say to each other without losing the essential characteristics of their beliefs. This has led to a reexamination of what is essential to each. Of course, the answers have varied from person to person, but the continuing dialogue may open up some extremely fruitful exchanges. At the minimum each one is learning about the other.

As can now be seen, Marxism and communism are complex, many-faceted ways of viewing the world. Communism as it is today has been treated as the logical extension of Marxism, and in many ways it is, but it must be remembered that we left Marx when we started discussing theories of the revolution and only returned to him with Full Communism. Contemporary communism is as much the product of Lenin, Stalin, Khrushchev, and Mao Tse-tung as it is of Marx, if not more so. The dictatorship of the proletariat was to be a fairly brief period of transition, and for all but a few it has become the final stage—a stage that will change certainly, but it will change internally, gradually being adjusted to the needs and desires of its leaders and the population that they rule rather than consciously driven on to a new stage. But the ideas of Marx have helped greatly to form the thinking of the men who have developed contemporary communism, and Marxism has helped to mold the thinking of those who rule today, and therefore it cannot be neglected. It is difficult to judge precisely the effect that Marx has had on the thinking of these men, but it seems obvious that the world is still viewed through Marx's eyes at least some of the time.

SUGGESTED READINGS

Marxism

Almond, Gabriel A.   *The Appeals of Communism.* Princeton, N.J.: Princeton University Press, 1954.

Aptheker, Herbert, ed.   *Marxism and Christianity; A Symposium.* New York: Humanities Press, 1968.

————.   *The Urgency of Marxist-Christian Dialogue.* New York: Harper & Row, 1970.

Avineri, Shlomo.   *The Social and Political Thought of Karl Marx.* Cambridge, Eng.: Cambridge University Press, 1968.

Brus, Wlodzimierz.   *The Economics and Politics of Socialism.* London: Routledge & Kegan Paul, 1974.

Burns, Emile.   *An Introduction to Marxism.* New York: International Publishers Co., 1966.

Coates, Ken.   *Essays on Socialist Humanism in Honour of the Centenary of Bertrand Russell 1872–1970.* Nottingham, Eng.: Spokesman Books, 1972.

Cohen, Arthur A.   *The Communism of Mao Tse-tung.* Chicago: University of Chicago Press, 1964.

Cole, G. D. H.   *The Meaning of Marxism.* Ann Arbor, Mich.: University of Michigan Press, 1948.

Curtis, Michael, ed.   *Marxism.* New York: Atherton Press, 1970.

De George, Richard T.   *The New Marxism. Soviet and European Marxism since 1956.* New York: Pegasus, 1968.

Devillers, Phillippe.   *What Mao Really Said.* Trans. Tony White. New York: Schocken Books, 1969.

Dunayevskaya, Raya.   *Marxism and Freedom from 1776 until Today.* London: Pluto Press, 1971.

Engels, Friedrich.   *Selected Writings.* Ed. W. O. Henderson. Baltimore: Penguin Books, 1967.

————.   *Socialism: Utopian and Scientific.* Any edition.

Fischer, Louis.   *The Life of Lenin.* New York: Harper & Row, 1964.

Franklin, Bruce, ed.   *The Essential Stalin; Major Theoretical Writings, 1905–1952.* Garden City, N.Y.: Doubleday & Co., 1972.

Fromm, Erich.   *Marx's Concept of Man.* New York: Frederick Ungar Publishing Co., 1966.

————, ed.   *Socialist Humanism; An International Symposium.* Garden City, N.Y.: Anchor Books, 1965.

Garaudy, Roger, and Lauer, Quentin, S. J.   *From Anathema to Dialogue; The Challenge of Marxist-Christian Cooperation.* London: Collins, 1967.

————. *A Christian-Communist Dialogue.* Garden City, N.Y.: Doubleday & Co., 1968.

————. *The Turning-Point of Socialism.* Trans. Peter Ross and Betty Ross. London: Fontana Books, 1970.

Girardi, Guilio. *Marxism and Christianity.* Trans. Keven Traynor. New York: Macmillan Co., 1968.

Gregor, A. James. *A Survey of Marxism; Problems in Philosophy and the Theory of History.* New York: Random House, 1965.

Gutnov, Alexei et al. *The Ideal Communist City.* Trans. Renee Neu Watkins. New York: George Braziller, 1968.

Gyorgy, Andrew, ed. *Issues of World Communism.* Princeton, N.J.: D. Van Nostrand Co., 1966.

Kolakowski, Leszek, and Hampshire, Stuart, eds. *The Socialist Idea: A Reappraisal.* London: Weidenfeld & Nicolson, 1974.

Lenin, V. I. *Imperialism; The Highest Stage of Capitalism.* New York: International Publishers Co., 1939.

————. *State and Revolution.* New York: International Publishers Co., 1943.

————. *What Is to Be Done?* New York: International Publishers, Co., 1943.

Leonard, Wolfgang. *Three Faces of Marxism; The Political Concepts of Soviet Ideology, Maoism, and Humanist.* Trans. Ewald Osers. New York: Holt, Rinehart, & Winston, 1974.

Lichtheim, George. *Marxism; An Historical and Critical Study.* 2d ed. New York: Frederick A. Praeger, 1965.

McLellan, David. *Karl Marx; His Life and Thought.* New York: Harper & Row, 1973.

Marković, Mihailo. *From Affluence to Praxis; Philosophy and Social Criticism.* Ann Arbor, Mich.: University of Michigan Press, 1974.

Marx, Karl. *Capital.* Any edition.

————. *Economic and Philosophic Manuscripts of 1844.* Trans. Martin Milligan. Moscow: Foreign Languages Publishing House, 1961.

————, and Engels, Friedrich. *The Communist Manifesto.* Any edition.

Mayo, Henry B. *Introduction to Marxist Theory.* New York: Oxford University Press, 1960.

Meszaros, Istvan. *Marx's Theory of Alienation.* London: Merlin Press, 1970.

Meyer, Alfred G. *Leninism.* New York: Frederick A. Praeger, 1962.

————. *Marxism; The Unity of Theory and Practice.* Ann Arbor, Mich.: University of Michigan Press, 1963.

————. *Communism.* 3d ed. New York: Random House, 1967.

Petrovic, Gajo. *Marx in the Mid-Twentieth Century; A Yugoslav Phi-*

losopher Considers Karl Marx's Writings. Garden City, N.J.: Anchor Books, 1967.

Schaff, Adam.   "Alienation as a Social and Philosophical Problem," *Social Praxis,* 3, # 1–2 (1975), pp. 7–26.

Schram, Stuart R.   *The Political Thought of Mao Tse-tung.* New York: Frederick A. Praeger, 1963.

Stojanovic, Svetozar.   *Between Ideals and Reality; A Critique of Socialism and Its Future.* Trans. Gerson S. Sher. New York: Oxford University Press, 1973.

Tucker, Robert C.   *Philosophy and Myth in Karl Marx.* Cambridge, Eng.: Cambridge University Press, 1961.

————.   *The Marxian Revolutionary Idea.* New York: W. W. Norton & Co., 1969.

Venable, Vernon.   *Human Nature; The Marxian View.* Cleveland, Ohio: World Publishing Co., 1966.

Wetter, Gustav A.   *Dialectical Materialsm; A Historical and Systematic Survey of Philosophy in the Soviet Union.* Trans. Peter Heath. New York: Frederick A. Praeger, 1958.

Zeitlin, Irving.   *Capitalism and Imperialism; An Introduction to Neo-Marxian Concepts.* Chicago: Markham & Co., 1972.

The Soviet Union

Bauer, Raymond A., and Inkeles, Alex.   *The Soviet Citizen: Daily Life in a Totalitarian Society.* Cambridge, Mass.: Harvard University Press, 1959.

————; and Kluckhohn, Clyde.   *How The Soviet System Works. Cultural, Psychological and Social Themes.* New York: Vintage Books, 1961.

Berman, Harold J.   *Justice in the U.S.S.R.* Rev. ed. New York: Vintage Books, 1963.

Bociurkiw, Bohdan R., and Strong, John W., eds.   *Religion and Atheism in the U.S.S.R. and Eastern Europe.* Toronto: University of Toronto Press, 1975.

Djilas, Milovan.   *The New Class. An Analysis of the Communist System.* New York: Frederick A. Praeger, 1957.

Katz, Abraham.   *The Politics of Economic Reform in the Soviet Union.* New York: Frederick A. Praeger, 1972.

Medvedev, Roy.   *On Socialist Democracy.* Trans. and ed. Ellen DeKadt. New York: Knopf, 1975.

Milivtin, N. A.   *Sotsgorod; The Problems of Building Socialist Cities.* Cambridge, Mass.: M.I.T. Press, 1975.

Osborn, Robert J.   *Soviet Social Policies: Welfare, Equality and Community.* Homewood, Ill.: Dorsey Press, 1970.

Rothberg, Abraham.   *The Heirs of Stalin; Dissidence and the Soviet*

Regime, 1953–1970. Ithaca, N.Y.: Cornell University Press, 1972.

Sakharov, Andrei D.   *My Country and the World.* Trans. Guy V. Daniels. New York: Knopf, 1975.

Simon, Gerhard.   *Church State and Opposition in the U.S.S.R.* London: Hurst, 1974.

Solzhenitsyn, Alexander.   *The Gulag Archipelago.* 3 vols. N.Y.: Harper & Row, 1974–77.

Talbott, Strobe, ed, and trans.   *Khrushchev Remembers.* Boston: Little, Brown & Co., 1970.

Tökés, Rudolf L., ed.   *Dissent in the U.S.S.R.; Politics, Ideology, and People.* Baltimore: Johns Hopkins University Press, 1975.

Wetter, Gustav.   *Soviet Ideology Today.* New York: Frederick A. Praeger, 1966.

China

Barnett, A. Doak.   *Communist China: The Early Years, 1949–1955.* New York: Frederick A. Praeger, 1964.

———.   *Cadres, Bureaucracy, and Political Power in Communist China.* New York: Columbia University Press, 1967.

Chang, Parris H.   *Power and Policy in China.* University Park, Pa.: Pennsylvania State University Press, 1975.

Chen, Jack.   *Inside the Cultural Revolution.* New York: Macmillan Co., 1975.

———.   *A Year in Upper Felicity; Life in a Chinese Village during the Cultural Revolution.* New York: Macmillan Co., 1973.

Deleyne, Jan.   *The Chinese Economy.* Trans. Robert Leriche. London: Deutsch, 1973.

Esmein, Jean.   *The Chinese Cultural Revolution.* Trans. W. F. J. Jenner. London: Deutsch, 1975.

Fairbank, John King.   *The United States and China.* Rev. ed. New York: Compass Books, 1962.

Geddes, W. R.   *Peasant Life in Communist China.* Ithaca, N.Y.: Society for Applied Anthropology, Cornell University, 1963.

Hinton, Harold C.   *Turning Point in China; An Essay on the Cultural Revolution.* New York: Monthly Review Press, 1972.

———.   *An Introduction to Chinese Politics.* New York: Frederick A. Praeger, 1973.

Hinton, William.   *Fanshen: A Documentary of Revolution in a Chinese Village.* New York: Monthly Review Press, 1967.

Karol, K. S.   *The Second Chinese Revolution.* Trans. Mervyn Jones. London: Jonathan Cape, 1975.

Lewis, John Wilson.   *Leadership in Communist China.* Ithaca, N.Y.: Cornell University Press, 1963.

————, ed.   *Major Doctrines of Communist China.* New York: W. W. Norton & Co., 1964.

Liu, William Thomas, ed.   *Chinese Society under Communism. A Reader.* New York: John Wiley & Sons, 1967.

Myrdal, Jan.   *Report from a Chinese Village.* Trans. Maurice Michael. New York: Pantheon Books, 1965.

Price, R. F.   *Education in Communist China.* Rev. ed. London: Routledge & Kegan Paul, 1976.

Robinson, Thomas W., ed.   *The Cultural Revolution in China.* Berkeley, Calif.: University of California Press, 1971.

Schram, Stuart R.   *Authority, Participation and Cultural Change in China.* Cambridge, Eng.: Cambridge University Press, 1973.

Skinner, G. William et al., eds.   *Modern Chinese Society: An Analytical Bibliography.* Stanford: Stanford University Press, 1973.

Snow, Edgar.   *The Other Side of the River: Red China Today.* New York: Random House, 1962.

Tsang, Chiu-sam.   *Society, Schools and Progress in China.* Oxford, Eng.: Pergamon Press, 1968.

Vogel, Ezra F.   *Canton under Communism: Programs and Politics in a Provincial Capital, 1949–1968.* Cambridge, Mass.: Harvard University Press, 1969.

Wang, James C. F.   *The Cultural Revolution in China: An Annotated Bibliography.* New York: Garland, 1976.

Yang, C. K.   *Religion in Chinese Society: A Study of Contemporary Social Functions of Religion and Some of Their Historical Factors.* Berkeley, Calif.: University of California Press, 1961.

————.   *Chinese Communist Society: The Family and the Village.* Cambridge, Mass.: M.I.T. Press, 1965.

Other Communist countries

Bicanić, Rudolf.   *Economic Policy in Socialist Yugoslavia.* Cambridge, Eng.: Cambridge University Press, 1973.

Nelson, Lowry.   *Cuba: The Meaning of a Revolution.* Minneapolis: University of Minnesota Press, 1972.

Silverman, Bertram, ed.   *Man and Socialism in Cuba; The Great Debate.* New York: Athenaeum, 1971.

5

Fascism and national socialism

For the generation that lived through World War II, the words *fascism, national socialism,* and *nazism* raise indescribably horrible pictures of brutality and inhumanity. For those who have grown up since the end of the war, the horror associated with the concentration camps has faded. Today many people use the word *Fascist* to describe anyone of conservative political view, any member of the establishment, or even anyone with whom they disagree. While attributing Fascist views to such people is almost always wrong, fascism and national socialism are not dead. In fact, they are reviving in many countries.

Fascism and national socialism are similar enough to be called one ideology. There are differences, but national socialism is more accurately seen as one of a number of varieties of fascism rather than different in kind. Furthermore, we tend to identify them with individual leaders—particularly we tend to identify Adolf Hitler with national socialism.

Although the discussion here is limited to the major movements in Germany and Italy during the period prior to World War II, it should be remembered that there are a number of countries in the world today that come close to the Fascist model.

THE THEORETICAL BASE

Any discussion of fascism and national socialism must emphasize eight basic concepts that are found in all Fascists and National Socialists. Although the concepts are given different emphases by different writers, they all exist in all the writers. They are:

1. Irrationalism.
2. Social Darwinism.
3. Nationalism.
4. The state.
5. The principle of leadership.
6. Racism (more important in national socialism than in fascism).
7. The corporate economy.
8. Anticommunism.

The first two concepts are best seen as basic themes that are rarely explicitly stated. All eight of these concepts are intimately interrelated, and the reader should avoid placing each in a separate compartment cut off from the others. But it is necessary to analyze them separately to understand them.

Irrationalism.[1] Irrationalism permeates the approach of fascism and national socialism but by its very nature it is difficult to analyze. Most importantly, irrationalism entails the rejection of the approach of the 19th century to social problems. This approach was fundamentally rationalist, whether Marxist or liberal-democratic. It saw identifiable social problems that could be solved by the application of reason and science. In opposition to this approach, fascism and national socialism reject the application of reason and science to social problems and use myth, appeal to the emotions, and hate as tools for manipulating man. The basic assumption is that humans are not rational beings. They need not be reasoned with and cannot be reasoned with; they can only be led and manipulated.

The emphasis for national socialism is on myths of blood (racism) and soil (nationalism) and on violence as a constant

---

[1] Irrationalism is also part of other ideologies, but it is most important in relationship to fascism and national socialism.

part of life. In particular, not only is violence something that is directed at the national and racial enemies, but it is also a normal aspect of political life. In this context, it should be noted that Germans who did not fit Hitler's image of racial purity were executed as well as Jews and others who were regularly attacked.

This is part of the appeal of fascism. For someone who is insecure, financially, socially, or emotionally, an appeal based on race hatred, intense nationalism, and the like, which promotes a feeling of worth as a member of a superior race or nation and identifies people who are believed to be inferior, can be very effective. Fascism gives a sense of belonging, a sense of superiority, and a sense of security to those who feel cut off, inferior, or insecure. And it does this in such a way that the feeling need not be questioned.

Social Darwinism.   Social Darwinism is the name generally given to social theories that view life as a struggle for survival within each species as well as between the species. In Charles Darwin's[2] book *On the Origin of Species by Means of Natural Selection* (1859), there is found the statement that life evolved through a struggle for survival *between* the species. The Social Darwinists took this idea and applied it to each species. In other words, rather than seeing a struggle for survival *between* the species, they saw a struggle for survival *within* the species.[3] Fascists and National Socialists applied this idea to their theories of nationalism and race, and we will return to it in that context.[4] It should be clear from the above that not all Social Darwinists are racists. Social Darwinism is a general theory that the Fascists and National Socialists applied to their theories.

Nationalism.   By far the most important theme, as illustrated in the phrase *national* socialism, is nationalism. In Chapter 2 we analyzed the basic characteristics of nationalism. Here we will try to see what they mean to the Fascist. A good beginning to

---

[2] Charles Darwin (1809–82). Famous English naturalist who put forth a number of important theses regarding evolution.

[3] A later thinker whom we will look at in the chapter on "Anarchism," Peter Kropotkin (1842–1921), argues in his book *Mutual Aid* (1902) that there is considerable evidence for cooperation within the species.

[4] For a further analysis of the role of Social Darwinism in national socialism, see Hajo Holborn, "Origins and Political Character of Nazi Ideology," *Political Science Quarterly*, vol. 74 (December 1964), pp. 542–54.

understanding nationalism in this context can be found in Hitler's statement, "I am deeply stirred by the word which Ulrich
Hutten wrote the last time he seized his pen:—Germany."[5]
Here we find the fundamental notion of nationalism as patriotism, or love of country, but, in fascism, nationalism is much
more than this simple statement. It takes on a much different
meaning, to the extent that some scholars call it by a modified
name, such as "integral" nationalism.[6]

The nation is the key unit to which the Fascist relates. For the
National Socialist, this position is most often taken by race, with
the nation as a secondary concern. For the Fascist, an individual is first and foremost a member of the nation to which he
gives all of his loyalty, his dedication, and his love. The individual cannot exist separate from his or her existence in the nation.
In this way, there is almost no such thing as an individual within
Fascist ideology. An individual is one small part of the nation.

This feeling of being part of the nation goes beyond Doob's
definition of nationalism. For the Fascist, nationalism does not
give rise to something within the individual; the individual and
the nation are inseparable. The individual should not be able
to conceive of himself or herself as something different from
existence in the nation. People should be completely wrapped
up in the nation. Therefore, they would be unable to conceive
of the nation going out of existence, and demands made on
this basis would seem rather pointless to them. Although not
all citizens of Fascist countries felt this strongly, it does illustrate
the ideal Fascist citizen. Fascist citizens would think like this
if they completely fitted the mold of the ideology. Certainly,
there will be very few individuals who completely fit that mold,
but one must remember again the underlying motif of the irrational in Fascist ideology, particularly since this love of nation,
this nationalism, was consciously used by the leadership to
mold the citizens as close to the model as possible. For the
Fascist the nation was the key to this molding. For the National
Socialist it was race, but it was race closely connected with
nation.

---

[5] Quoted in A. P. Laurie, *The Case for Germany: A Study of Modern Germany* (Berlin: Internationaler Verlag, 1939), p. 2.

[6] See, for example, Carlton J. H. Hayes, *The Historical Evolution of Modern
Nationalism* (New York: Macmillan Co., 1931), pp. 164–231.

For the National Socialist, nationalism was usually so closely connected with racism that it formed one concept rather than two. This is neatly illustrated by the following directive to all German schools:

> Teachers are directed to instruct their pupils in "the nature, causes, and effects of all racial and hereditary problems," to bring home to them the importance of race and heredity for the life and destiny of the German people, and to awaken in them a sense of their responsibility toward "the community of the nation" (their ancestors, the present generation, and posterity), pride in their membership of the German race as a foremost vehicle of hereditary Nordic values, and the will consciously to cooperate in the racial purification of the German stock. Racial instruction is to begin with the youngest pupils (six years of age) in accordance with the desire of the Führer "that no boy or girl should leave school without complete knowledge of the necessity and meaning of blood purity."[7]

Here we see the intimate connection in Nazi thought between racism and nationalism, and we see an explicit attempt to use the educational system to give children the value system of the ideology.

But, for the Fascist in general, racism is not closely connected to nationalism. In fact, racism, although part of the Fascist outlook, played a fairly minor role in both ideology and practice in a number of countries, such as Italy. In other countries with Fascist groups today, racism is an important part of the ideology. The United States is one of these countries with a number of small groups that are either National Socialist or Fascist and racist.

Nonracist fascism does hold a strongly nationalist position, but it is usually presented in connection with the concept of the state. The following statement by Mussolini is a good example: "The key-stone of the Fascist doctrine is the conception of the State, of its essence, of its functions, its aims. For Fascism the State is absolute, individuals and groups relative."[8] Musso-

---

[7] Quoted in *The Times* (London), 29 January 1935, p. 12. Reproduced from *The Times* by permission. Also reprinted in George L. Mosse, *Nazi Culture: Intellectual, Cultural and Social Life in the Third Reich* (New York: Grosset & Dunlap, 1966), pp. 282–84.

[8] Benito Mussolini, "The Doctrine of Fascism," in Mussolini, *Fascism; Doctrine and Institutions* (New York: Howard Fertig, 1968), p. 27.

lini continues in the same vein, contending that the state is the
carrier of the culture and spirit of the people or nation; that it
is the past, present, and future; that it represents the "imma-
nent conscience of the nation"; and that it educates the citizens
in all the virtues.[9] Here is clearly stated the connection between
the state and nationalism in Fascist ideology. Mussolini's statements on the role of the state illustrate that the state should be
seen as the physical embodiment of the spirit of the nation. The
state is that entity which brings together the ideas and ideals
that form the basis of nationalism. Nationalism and the notion
of the state cannot be easily separated for the Fascist. The state,
as Mussolini said, is the carrier of the culture and spirit of the
people. The state is the driving force that welds together the
people. The state is capable of focusing the spirit of the people and the nationalism of the country. The state therefore
must be strong. The state must have the power necessary to
achieve those goals.

The state.   The role of the state is also significant by itself.
The state is the vehicle through which the attributes of the nation, nationality, or the race are expressed. But, to understand
the distinction they make, it should be noted that the state, at
least as viewed by Hitler, is a "rigid formal organization," and
the nation or the people is a "living organism," which must
replace the state.[10] The theory of the state as actually presented
by Fascists and National Socialists combines these two notions
into the idea of an organic[11] or corporate state.

This conception of the state stresses the continuity over the
generations of the entire society. The word *organic* means that
"social groups as fractions of the species receive thereby a life
and scope which transcends the scope and life of the individuals identifying themselves with the history and finalities of the
uninterrupted series of generations."[12] Put somewhat differently,

---

[9]Ibid., pp. 27–28.

[10] Adolf Hitler, *The Speeches of Adolf Hitler, April 1922–August 1939,* ed.
Norman H. Baynes (London: Oxford University Press, 1942), vol. I, p. 178.
Speech of September 1930.

[11] Some Fascists reject the idea that they are presenting the "organic the-
ory of the state." See, for example, Alfredo Rocco, "The Political Doctrine of
Fascism," in *Readings on Fascism and National Socialism* (Denver, Colo.: Alan
Swallow, Publisher, n.d.), p. 34.

[12] Ibid.

this means that the society, represented by the state, is a separate entity having a life or existence at once different from, and more than, the life of any individual within that society. This also means that the life of the individual is less important than the life of the society.

This point, which we have mentioned before, is best illustrated by the idea of the folkish state that we find expressed by Hitler in *Mein Kampf:*

> Thus, the highest purpose of a *folkish* state is concern for the preservation of those original racial elements which bestow culture and create the beauty and dignity of a higher humanity. We, as Aryans, can conceive of the state only as the living organism of a nationality which not only assures the preservation of this nationality, but by the development of its spiritual and ideal abilities leads it to the highest freedom.[13]

The folkish state is the best symbol that one can find for the full idea of the identification of the individual with the mass. Here we have the ideas of blood and soil intermingled in a way that illustrates why they are so important to national socialism. The folkish state is a racial state. It is a state in which only the members of the true Aryan race may participate, but they participate only in the sense of giving of themselves to the state. They do not participate in any sense of governing. The folkish state, then, is a state based on racial purity. Furthermore, it is a state based on ideas of soil, myths of racial content, but connected with the particular history of the German nation in this case. Here we have race and nationalism, blood and soil, combined in the notion of the folkish state. It is clear, therefore, that an understanding of national socialism as it developed in Germany cannot be separated from an understanding of race, nationalism, and the combination of the two in a folkish state.

There is a difference of emphasis between Fascist and National Socialist conceptions of the state. For example, Mussolini specifically rejects Hitler's position that the nation is prior to the state. He does this simply by arguing that the nation cannot exist without the state to weld together the disparate masses into a nation. Mussolini says that the state is the source of the

[13] Adolf Hitler, *Mein Kampf,* trans., Ralph Manheim (Boston: Houghton Mifflin Co., 1943), p. 394. Emphasis in the original.

life of the people of all generations that compose it.[14] The state is owed supreme loyalty by the individuals who live within it at any particular time, but the state is also something more than these somewhat mechanical notions imply. The state is also a "spiritual" unit, but this "spiritual" side is closely related to the authority that controls the state at any given time. The state "enforces discipline and uses authority, entering into the soul and ruling with undisputed sway."[15] This is, of course, the leadership principle.

The leadership principle. The state is the mechanism for enforcing the Fascist beliefs, and the state is run on the leadership or *Führer* principle which states that each subordinate owes absolute obedience to his immediate superior, with everyone ultimately subordinate to the absolute leader, the *Führer*. This hierarchy of leaders with a single, absolute leader at the top is an important characteristic of fascism and national socialism, although it should be noted that the underlying theory contends that the *Führer* is not absolute. But the only limit on his power, even in the theory, is that he must reflect the collective will of the people. This in no way actually limits the power of the leader even in the theory because his will is defined as being the same as the collective will. "His will is not the subjective, individual will of a single man, but the collective national will."[16] The leader's authority, therefore, in national socialism and, for the same reason, in fascism is absolute. In practice he has also usually been what we call a charismatic leader, one who is able to attract people by the sheer force of his personality. Because of this fact few fascist movements have survived the death of the leader.

The *Führer* principle on which Hitler based his power and organization seems, on the surface, to be somewhat complicated, but, if we remember the discussion of representation in the chapter on democracy, we will recall the notion of the representative as embodying within himself the will of his constituency. This is what is meant by the *Führer* principle. Hitler,

---

[14] Mussolini, "The Doctrine of Fascism," pp. 11–12.

[15] Ibid., p. 14.

[16] Ernst Rudolf Huber, *Verfassungsrecht des grossdeutschen Reiches* (Hamburg, 1939), p. 195; trans. and quoted in *Readings on Fascism and National Socialism*, p. 75.

as leader, is the representative of the German nation and of the Aryan race in the sense that he embodies within himself all the aspirations of the people. It should be clear that this does not mean that Hitler follows the will of the people, but that he, by embodying their will, is capable of *rightly* interpreting it. This is the clue to the whole notion of the *Führer* principle—the *Führer* is the only one who is capable of rightly interpreting the will of the people. When the *Führer* speaks, he speaks as the representative of what the people truly want. In this sense he must be considered to be virtually infallible, and this is clearly how Hitler viewed himself. Hitler as *Führer* could not err.

But one man cannot rule an entire country, even if his will is the embodiment of the collective will of the people of that country, and therefore even an absolute ruler needs some apparatus to enforce his rules. This apparatus is found in the party. Party members are the most direct participants in the leader-follower relationship defined above, and they all are apart from and above the population as a whole. They are also normally identified by some clearly recognizable sign, such as a uniform. Finally, there is often an elite corps within this elite which serves in part to check on the rest of the party. The two groups that served this function within the National Socialist German Workers Party (the official name of Hitler's party) were the S.A. (*Sturmabteilung*) and the S.S. (*Schutzstaffel*). Hitler defined the task of the S.A. as follows:

> The SA on behalf of our German people must educate the young German in mind and body so that he becomes a man hard as steel and ready to fight.
> Out of hundreds of thousands of individuals it must forge one united, disciplined, mighty organization.
> In the age of Democracy and authority of the Leader, in the period of unbridled freedom, iron discipline, must be the foundation of the S.A.[17]

This statement is also illustrative of the role of the entire party. It is expected to obey without question, and its primary task is to educate the entire population in the correct principles of life.

---

[17] Adolf Hitler, "Introduction to the Service-Order of the S.A.," quoted in Hitler, *Speeches*, vol. 1, p. 169. By permission of the Oxford University Press.

Under Hitler the party is the effective ruling mechanism. As Hitler said:

> The function of the Party is:
>
> 1. The building up of its own internal organization so as to create a stable, self-renewing, permanent cell of National Socialist teaching.
> 2. The education of the entire people in the meaning of the conceptions of this idea.
> 3. The introduction of those who have been so trained into the State to serve either as leaders or followers.[18]

But lest there be any mistake as to what this means, he also says, "every member of the Party has to do what the leader orders."[19]

The party in fascism and national socialism played a role similar to that of the Communist party in Lenin's thought. The party was seen as the vanguard of the nation or the race rather than the proletariat, but the general notion is the same. The party is the forerunner of the new order to come. For the Nationalist Socialist as opposed to the Fascist, the new order is based on race.

Racism. Probably the single, best known part of national socialism is its racism. Hitler's refusal to award the Olympic gold medal to the Negro athlete Jesse Owens in the 1936 Olympics in Berlin is a well-known example of this attitude. Everyone also knows of the killing of 6 million Jews.

Hitler bases racism originally on the right of the stronger,[20] and he believed that from the very beginning the Aryan, or Nordic, or white, or sometimes German, race dominated all others. He contended that this domination was good for all because it was natural and founded on reason, and also that it was ultimately accepted gladly by the dominated races.[21]

Here we have clearly stated the thesis of the struggle for survival among the races. It is noteworthy that Hitler believed that racial domination by the Aryans would gladly be accepted by

---

[18] Hitler, *Speeches*, vol. 1, p. 444. Speech of 1935. By permission of the Oxford University Press.

[19] Ibid., p. 459. Speech of May 21, 1930.

[20] Hitler, *Speeches*, vol. 1, p. 465. Speech of January 15, 1936.

[21] Ibid., pp. 465–66.

the dominated races. This clearly is rationalization of his basic belief. The Darwinian notion of struggle for survival as interpreted by the National Socialist does not include the survival of the dominated races. The logic of the position is that the inferior races will be eliminated, not merely dominated. The only situation in which the dominated races could in fact continue to exist would be the situation in which it was felt that certain menial tasks required races lower than the Aryans to fulfill them.

Again, we should be very careful to note the role that racism plays in national socialism. It represents (1) the underlying current of Social Darwinism and (2) it was a mechanism of social control negatively by destroying the Jews and thus instilling fear in the Germans and positively by instilling a pride in the Germans in their so-called racial heritage. The racial policies of Hitler were not limited to extermination and breeding. They extended to the belief that all that is good in culture stems from the Aryan race and that, therefore, the Germans as the representative of the Aryans had the best cultural heritage of the Western world and would have an even better culture in the future. In the chapter on nationalism we noted that one of Hitler's great loves was Wagner. This was true because Wagner's operas were in some ways operas of the folkish state. They represented the myths of blood and soil that were so important to national socialism. Most importantly, they represented what Hitler saw as a high point in German culture—an illustration that the Germans did in fact have a great culture and particularly that Wagner, as a representative of German culture, seemed to agree in large part with the ideas put forth by Hitler. Therefore, Hitler could present national socialism as a logical outgrowth of German culture and the German nation.

The relationship of the state to racism is seen in the following extract from *Mein Kampf:*

> The state is a means to an end. Its end lies in the preservation and advancements of a community of physically and psychically homogeneous creatures. This preservation itself comprises first of all existence as a race and thereby permits the free development of all the forces dormant in this race. Of them a part will always primarily serve the preservation of physical life, and only

the remaining part the promotion of a further spiritual development. Actually the one always creates the precondition for the
other.[22]

The effects of racism on other aspects of the society are
fairly simple and obvious. For example, social stratification
would be based on racial purity and party membership. Other
things that would be taken into account would be positive support for the regime and contributions to the country. In addition, the racist ideology would dictate the control of marriage,
and the desire to control the minds of the children would dictate control of the family system. Along these lines, the German
woman was encouraged to have many children; that is, if she
was of the correct racial type. As Goebbels put it, "The mission
of woman is to be beautiful and to bring children into the
world."[23] She is also supposed to be athletic and refrain from
wearing makeup or from such things as smoking in public. But,
above all, she is to have children. We have seen the way in
which the educational system was used to develop the correct
values in the children. The family and religion were used in the
same way. Parents were supposed to teach their children the
true National Socialist ideas from birth. National socialism also
contended that it was supported by God, and thus religion was
used for the same purpose.

The corporate economy.   The final part of the ideology is
the most difficult to treat because the theory is inconsistent.
Even though socialism is part of the name national socialism
and Mussolini was originally a socialist, neither fascism nor national socialism was actually socialist. National socialism began
from that position, but it quickly changed as it gained the support of capitalists.[24] Probably the best statement of the general
economic theory is Huber's:

> All property is common property. The owner is bound by the
> people and the Reich to the responsible management of his

[22] Hitler, *Mein Kampf*, p. 393.

[23] Joseph Goebbels, quoted in Mosse, *Nazi Culture*, p. 41.

[24] On this point see Martin Broszat, *German National Socialism 1919–1945*,
trans. Kurt Rosenbaum and Inge Pauli Boehm (Santa Barbara, Calif.: CLIO
Press, 1966), pp. 22–24.

goods. His legal position is only justified when he satisfies this responsibility to the community.[25]

Thus, property under national socialism was held in private hands, but it had to be used as the government dictated or it would be confiscated. This is the corporate economy.

Here again we have the idea of the people as a whole acting for unity. A major concern in the economic theory is to establish economic self-sufficiency. For fascism and national socialism to achieve their goals, the countries must be self-sufficient, they must not depend on other countries for supplies.[26] This point is fairly obvious; all of the stress on the nation, the state, the race, and so on, would lose considerable force if they were dependent on other nations, states, races, and so forth.

The economic system of national socialism clearly states that, even though an individual may have temporary control of some economic good, be it land or capital or whatever, this control must serve the interests of the collectivity as interpreted by the *Führer* or the control must be terminated.

The economic system of fascism as distinct from that of national socialism includes the idea of state-controlled syndicates. The state creates all economic organizations as the Labour Charter of April 21, 1927 says:

> Work in all its forms—intellectual, technical and manual— both organizing or executive, is a social duty. On this score and only on this score, it is protected by the State.
> From the national standpoint the mass of production represents a single unit; it has a single object, namely, the well-being of individuals and the development of national power.[27]

All economic organization under fascism is ultimately controlled by the state. All economic organizations under fascism are designed to include both workers and employers in the same organization so that all of the economy can be directly

---

[25] Huber, *Verfassungsrecht,* pp. 327–73, quoted in *Readings on Fascism,* p. 91.

[26] See the discussion in Paul M. Hayes, *Fascism* (London: George Allen & Unwin, 1973), pp. 89–105.

[27] "The Labour Charter," in Benito Mussolini, *Four Speeches on the Corporate State* (Rome: "Laboremus," 1935), p. 53.

controlled from above. In this way the state is made clearly superior to every part of the economy. The syndicates are designed to ensure that production continues as long as the state requires it. The right to strike is taken away from the workers, but at the same time the syndicate operating as an arm of the state usually has the power to set wages; thus the syndicate acts as a policy-making arm of the state in economic affairs. It should be clear that, as in Germany, the Fascist party in Italy with Mussolini at the head had ultimate power. In many ways, the syndicates were merely administrative arms of the Fascist party and of Mussolini rather than having any real power to make decisions. The leadership principle was not abrogated in Italy. It was maintained, and the syndicates acted as lower level leaders following the dictates of the leader.

Anticommunism. One of the aspects of the ideologies of fascism and national socialism that made them acceptable to many was their anticommunist stance. As one scholar of fascism put it, "Before all else, it was anticommunist. It lived and throve on anticommunism."[28] In a large part this was an aspect of fascism's antirationalist approach, and its general rejection of the modern world. But it became a significant element in the appeal of fascism to many groups.[29]

Communists argue that the ideology's anticommunism is the only defining characteristic and that fascism should not be considered an ideology at all, but merely a reaction to the events of the early 20th century, particularly the development of an organized working class. While this interpretation has its merits, it misses the complexity of fascism and national socialism.

Fascism and national socialism were not only anticommunist, but also antiintellectual, antirational, and antimodern. As the Communists argue, much of the ideologies of fascism and national socialism developed first as practice and were never tightly tied together by theory. But the very lack of rational coherence can be seen as an integral part of the ideologies and

[28] H. R. Trevor-Roper, "The Phenomenon of Fascism," in S. J. Woolf (ed.) *European Fascism* (New York: Vintage Books, 1969), p. 24.

[29] See, for example, Alastair Hamilton, *The Appeal of Fascism; A Study of Intellectuals and Fascism 1919–1945* (New York: Avon Books, 1971).

part of the rejection of what was seen as the overly intellectual, overly rational approach of communism.

THE CURRENT SCENE

Evidence regarding the current status of fascism and national socialism around the world is spotty to say the least. One often reads of the resurgence of these movements in Germany and Japan, and, until the assassination of George Lincoln Rockwell, the Nazi party in the United States received considerable press coverage, even though its membership was very small. It is beginning to reappear in some areas now.

The greatest difficulty in analyzing the current situation stems from the tendency for movements to reject the labels of fascism or national socialism and for the number of adherents to be relatively small and thus not attract much attention. They seem, therefore, to be unimportant. At the same time, we must remember that the movements founded by Hitler and Mussolini began in obscurity and were small for many years. Thus, one cannot say with any certainty that a major Fascist or National Socialist movement is impossible. One can only say that such a movement is unlikely without conditions being present that give rise to considerable unrest, dissatisfaction, and demands for order. Such conditions obviously do exist in some countries, including the United States. It is possible that popular leaders could rise in any number of countries and achieve success through National Socialist or Fascist movements whether or not the actual label was used.

For such a movement to be successful, it will clearly require something more than simply dissatisfaction and demands for order. It will require an issue with great emotional content. This issue is present today in the United States in the question of race. Other issues can be made to have such emotional content with the appropriate type of leader. Thus, it would be a mistake to think of national socialism and fascism as dead, even though no major movements seem to exist.

In conclusion, I would like to simply quote from a recent survey of fascism. "Fascism and Nazism are still with us. Regimes and organizations inspired by them, or using the methods they have made all too famous, are still operating in all the five continents."[30]

SUGGESTED READINGS

Baumont, Maurice; Fried, John H. E.; and Vermeil, Edmond, eds.   *The Third Reich*. New York: Frederick A. Praeger, 1954.

Bell, Leland.   *In Hitler's Shadow: The Anatomy of American Nazism*. Port Washington, N.Y.: Kennikat Press, 1973.

Blanksten, George I.   *Peron's Argentina*. New York: Russell & Russell, 1953.

Broszat, Martin.   *German National Socialism 1919–1945*. Trans. Kurt Rosenbaum and Inge Pauli Boehm. Santa Barbara, Calif.: CLIO Press, 1966.

Carocci, Giampiero.   *Italian Fascism*. Trans. Isabel Quigly. Harmondsworth: Penguin, 1974.

Carsten, F. L.   *The Rise of Fascism*. Berkeley, Calif.: University of California Press, 1967.

Chadbod, Federico.   *A History of Italian Fascism*. London: Weidenfeld, 1963.

Del Boca, Angelo, and Giovana, Mario.   *Fascism Today; A World Survey*. Trans. R. H. Boothroyd. New York: Pantheon Books, 1969.

Fest, Joachim C.   *The Face of the Third Reich; Portraits of the Nazi Leadership*. Trans. Michael Bullock. New York: Pantheon Books, 1970.

———.   *Hitler*. Trans. Richard and Clara Winston. New York: Harcourt Brace Jovanovich, 1974.

Gregor, A. James.   *Fascism: The Classic Interpretations of the Interwar Period*. Morristown, N.J.: General Learning Press, 1973.

———.   *Fascism: The Contemporary Interpretations*. Morristown, N.J.: General Learning Press, 1973.

———.   *The Ideology of Fascism; The Rationale of Totalitarianism*. New York: Free Press, 1969.

Hamilton, Alastair.   *The Appeal of Fascism; A Study of Intellectuals and Fascism, 1919–1945*. New York: Macmillan Co., 1971.

Harris, Henry Silton.   *The Social Philosophy of Giovanni Gentile*. Urbana, Ill.: University of Illinois Press, 1960.

Hayes, Paul M.   *Fascism*. London: George Allen & Unwin Ltd., 1973.

---

[30] Angelo Del Boca and Mario Giovana, *Fascism Today; A World Survey*, trans. R. H. Boothroyd (New York: Pantheon Books, 1969), p. 428. Also see Christopher Seton-Watson, "Fascism in Contemporary Europe," in S. J. Woolf, ed., *European Fascism* (New York: Vintage Books, 1968), pp. 337–53.

Hitler, Adolf. *My New Order.* New York: Reynal & Hitchcock, 1941.

———. *The Speeches of Adolf Hitler, April 1922–August 1939.* Ed. Norman H. Baynes. 2 vols. London: Oxford University Press, 1942.

———. *Mein Kampf.* Trans. Ralph Manheim. Boston: Houghton Mifflin Co., 1943.

Joes, Anthony J. "Fascism: The Past and the Future," *Comparative Political Studies* (April 1974), pp. 107–33.

Kitchen, Martin. *Fascism.* London: Macmillan, 1976.

Kuper, Leo, ed. *Race, Science and Society.* London: George Allen & Unwin, 1975.

Laqueur, Walter, ed. *Fascism: A Reader's Guide.* Berkeley: University of California Press, 1976.

Laurie, A. P. *The Case for Germany; A Study of Modern Germany.* Berlin: Internationaler Verlag, 1939.

Lyttelton, Adrian, ed. *Italian Fascisms. From Pareto to Gentile.* Trans. Douglas Parmée. London: Jonathan Cape, 1973.

Mosse, George L. *The Crisis of German Ideology; Intellectual Origins of the Third Reich.* New York: Grosset & Dunlap, 1964.

———. *Nazi Culture: Intellectual, Cultural and Social Life in the Third Reich.* New York: Grosset & Dunlap, 1966.

Mussolini, Benito. *My Autobiography.* New York: Charles Scribner's Sons, 1928.

———. *Four Speeches on the Corporate State.* Rome: "Laboremus," 1935.

———. *The Corporate State.* Florence, Italy: Vallecchi, 1936.

———. *Fascism; Doctrine and Institutions.* New York: Howard Fertig, 1968.

Neumann, Franz. *Behemoth: The Structure and Practice of National Socialism.* 2d ed. New York: Octagon Books, 1963.

Nolte, Ernst. *Three Faces of Fascism: Action Française, Italian Fascism, National Socialism.* Trans. Leila Vennewitz. New York: Holt, Rinehart & Winston, 1965.

Payne, Stanley G. *Falange; A History of Spanish Fascism.* Stanford, Calif.: Stanford University Press, 1961.

Readings on Fascism and National Socialism. Denver, Colo.: Alan Swallow, Publisher, n.d.

Reich, Wilhelm. *The Mass Psychology of Fascism.* Trans. Vincent R. Carfagno. New York: Farrar, Strauss & Giroux, 1970.

Rocco, Alfredo. "The Political Doctrine of Fascism," Trans. D. Bigongiari, *International Conciliation,* no. 223 (October 1926), pp. 393–415.

Smith, Dennis Mack. *Mussolini's Roman Empire.* New York: Viking Press, 1976.

Speer, Albert.   *Inside the Third Reich: Memoirs*. Trans. Richard Winston and Clara Winston. New York: Macmillan Co., 1970.

Stephenson, Jill.   *Women in Nazi Society*. London: Croom, Helm, 1975.

Taylor, Robert P.   *The Word in Stone; The Role of Architecture in the National Socialist Ideology*. Berkeley: University of California Press, 1975.

Theories of Fascism, Journal of Contemporary History, 11 (October 1976), entire issue.

Turner, Henry A., Jr., ed.   *Reappraisals of Fascism*. New York: New Viewpoints, 1975.

Viereck, Peter.   *Metapolitics; The Roots of the Nazi Mind*. Rev. ed. New York: Capricorn Books, 1961.

Weber, Eugen.   *Varieties of Fascism; Doctrines of Revolution in the Twentieth Century*. Princeton, N.J.: D. Van Nostrand Co., 1964.

Weiss, John.   *The Fascist Tradition; Radical Right-Wing Extremism in Modern Europe*. New York: Harper & Row, 1967.

Woolf, S. J., ed.   *European Fascism*. New York: Vintage Books, 1968.

————.   *The Nature of Fascism*. London: Weidenfeld & Nicolson, 1968.

Zeman, Z. A. B.   *Nazi Propaganda*. 2d ed. New York: Oxford University Press, 1973.

6

Anarchism

The visibility of anarchism as an ideology has varied throughout this century. At one time *anarchism* was a household word in the United States, in the same way that *communism* is today. Because of the fear with which they were viewed at the beginning of the 20th century, anarchists became the only group restricted from immigration into the United States on the basis of political beliefs. At other times, including the period from about 1930 into the 1960s, little was heard of anarchism; it seemed to be a dead issue. On the other hand, the 1970s has demonstrated considerable interest in and popularity of anarchist thought. Students rioting in Paris in June 1968, carried the anarchist banner, not the Communist, and the black flag of anarchism is now frequently seen in demonstrations and protests. It is generally accepted that the New Left and the new communal movement are closely related to anarchism. In the United States, libertarianism, or minimalism, has been very popular and is closely associated with various forms of anarchism. It can be said that anarchism is again a living ideology. Although it is not as strong at present as it was a few years ago, it seems to be revitalized in much of the world.

PRINCIPLES OF ANARCHISM

The ideology that we call anarchism has a wide variety of forms and includes a number of different ideas. The purpose of this chapter will be to explore the principles of anarchism in an effort to understand both the appeal of anarchism and the reaction against it. Most studies of anarchism have focused on a select group of men; Prince Peter Kropotkin (1842–1921), Pierre-Joseph Proudhon (1809–65), Mikhail Bakunin (1814–76), Count Leo Tolstoi (1828–1910), Max Stirner (1806–56), William Godwin (1756–1836), and William Morris (1834–96), with sometimes a bow in the direction of a few lesser known figures such as Errico Malatesta (1850–1932), Elisée Reclus (1830–1905), Benjamin Tucker (1854–1939), and Josiah Warren (1798?–1874). This approach may produce a valid presentation and analysis of the clusters of ideas that make up anarchism, but it is equally likely to result in a misunderstanding of the important similarities and the equally important differences among anarchists. The best approach, therefore, seems to be to select those parts of the anarchist tradition that are most important today while striving to maintain a balanced presentation.

Kropotkin once defined anarchism as:

> the name given to a principle or theory of life and conduct under which society is conceived without government—harmony in such a society being obtained, not by submission to law or by obedience to any authority, but by free agreements concluded between the various groups, territorial and professional, freely constituted for the sake of production and consumption, as also for the satisfaction of the infinite variety of needs and aspirations of a civilized being.[1]

Anarchism is, then, a political philosophy which holds that no group in society should have coercive authority over the society as a whole, and, on the positive side, that society should be composed of a wide variety of groups designed to coordinate the functions that are essential to the operation of any society. Anarchists differ somewhat on the interrelationships among these groups and on the importance of particular groups in the social system, but they would agree, with some reservations, with this definition. As another anarchist, Alexander Berkman (1870–1936), stated, "Anarchism teaches that we can live in a society where there is no compulsion of any kind. A life with-

---

[1] Peter Kropotkin, "Anarchism," *Encyclopaedia Britannica*, 11th ed., vol. I, p. 914.

out compulsion naturally means liberty; it means freedom from being forced or coerced, a chance to lead the life that suits you best."[2] This characterization gives, I think, a clue both to the appeal of anarchism and to the hate and fear of it. Anarchism gives us a picture of a peaceful, free life, one without many rules and regulations that appear so often to be designed simply to keep you from doing what seems right to you. Such a vision is very appealing, but it also attacks the foundations of modern society, government, the church, and the family. So it is hated and feared and many believe that it would bring chaos rather than the peaceful, noncoercive society of the vision.

The basic assumption of anarchism is that coercion or power exercised by one person over another is the cause of most of our contemporary problems. As one anarchist says, "Many people say that government is necessary because some men cannot be trusted to look after themselves, but anarchists say that government is harmful because no man can be trusted to look after anyone else."[3] All anarchists would agree with this statement. They all focus on the corrupting nature of power, and they believe that human beings are capable of organizing their affairs without anyone exercising authority over others. This does not mean that there will be no order in society, but that people can and will cooperatively produce a better system than can be produced by any authority. "Given a common need, a collection of people will, by trial and error, by improvisation and experiment, evolve order out of chaos—this order being more durable than any kind of externally imposed order."[4] And this order, this organization, will be better designed to fit human needs than any imposed one could possibly be because it will be "(1) voluntary, (2) functional, (3) temporary, and (4) small."[5]

Each of the above points is important for an understanding of anarchism. First, basic to all anarchism is the voluntary na-

[2] Alexander Berkman, *ABC of Anarchism,* 3d ed. (London: Freedom Press, 1964), p. 10.

[3] Nicolas Walter, *About Anarchism* (London: Freedom Press, 1969), p. 6. Originally published as *Anarchy 100,* vol. 9 (June 1969).

[4] Colin Ward, "Anarchism as a Theory of Organization," *Anarchy 62,* vol. 6 (April 1966), p. 103.

[5] Ibid., p. 101. See also, Terry Phillips, "Organization—The Way Forward," *Freedom,* vol. 31 (August 22, 1970), p. 3.

ture of any association. Second, an association should develop only to fill a fairly specific need and thus should be designed to fill that need alone. Therefore, third, it would disappear after the need was met. Finally, it must be small enough so that the people can control it rather than being controlled by it. This type of organization can be seen in the food cooperatives that have recently appeared around the country. They are voluntary; they serve to provide better food at lower prices than are otherwise available; they last only as long as needed; and they are small enough to be controlled by the members without a hierarchy of officers who need to be given power. They are a good example of how anarchists would like to organize all of society.

This rejection of authority and the feeling that it is possible to replace a coercive society with voluntary cooperation is about the only thing anarchists agree upon, and there are undoubtedly a few who would want to modify this statement. But "the essence of anarchism, the one thing without which it is not anarchism, is the negation of authority over anyone by anyone."[6]

Beyond this anarchism divides loosely into two categories; (1) collectivist with emphasis on the individual within a voluntary association of individuals, and (2) individualist with emphasis on the individual separate from any association. The former is sometimes divided into Communist anarchist and anarcho-syndicalists; the latter is usually divided into individualist anarchists and anarcho-capitalists, also known as minimalists or libertarians. In each case, though, the similarities are more important than the differences.

COLLECTIVIST ANARCHISM

Communist anarchism, traditionally associated primarily with Kropotkin, is the most developed and comprehensive anarchist theory. It starts, as does all anarchism, with the assumption that coercion in any form is bad. It suggests as the solution to the problem of order in a society without a government that there be established a series of small, voluntary communes or col-

---

[6] Walter, *About Anarchism*, p. 8.

lectives. These communes would join together into a federation for whatever common needs there were. As George Woodcock stated, "The village would appoint delegates to the regional federations, which in their turn would appoint delegates to the national federations. No delegate would have the power to speak for anything but the decisions of the workers who elected him,[7] and would be subject to recall at any time."[8] He goes on to say the delegate would be elected for a short period of time, and although expenses might be paid, the delegate would receive exactly the same salary as if still working at his or her regular job.[9]

Anarcho-syndicalists take essentially the same approach, except that they refer specifically to the work situation, particularly industrial work. The basic principles are as follows:

1. Each industry is organized into a federation of independent communes.
2. Each industry is controlled by the workers in that industry.[10]
3. Policy questions and questions of intercommune relations are handled by a coordinating council.

The key to an understanding of anarcho-syndicalism is found in its industrial base. The central element of anarcho-syndicalism is workers' control. The society is organized on the basis of the control of each industry by the workers in that industry. The word *industry* is normally defined quite broadly by the anarcho-syndicalists to include such activities as the building industry, which then would be controlled by all of the different workers who participate in building any structure. (Figure 6–1 is a representation of the planned organization of the Industrial Workers of the World illustrating this point.) Thus, these individuals meet to resolve the particular problems of that industry. Then representatives of each industry assemble to administer the

---

[7] This should remind one of the discussion of representation in Chapter 3.

[8] George Woodcock, *New Life to the Land* (London: Freedom Press, 1942), p. 26.

[9] On this point, see also, P. S., "Anarcho-Syndicalism—The Workers Next Step," *Freedom*, vol. 26 (January 30, 1965), p. 4.

[10] There is a vast literature on workers' control. For a sampling see Ken Coates and Tony Topham, eds., *Workers' Control* (London: Panther Books, 1970); *Anarchy 2*, vol. 1 (April 1961); G. D. H. Cole, *Workshop Organization* (London: Hutchinson Educational, 1973); and Cole, *Self-Government in Industry* (London: Hutchinson Educational, 1972).

FIGURE 6–1

The One Big Union Structure

of the

INDUSTRIAL WORKERS of the WORLD

A labor organization to correctly represent the working class must have two things in view.

First — It must combine the wage-workers in such a way that it can most successfully fight the battles and protect the interests of the working class in their struggle for shorter hours, more wages and better job conditions.

Second — It must offer a final solution of the labor problem — an emancipation from strikes, jails and scabbing.

Study the chart and observe how this organization provides the means for control of shop affairs, provides perfect industrial unionism, and converges the strength of all organized workers to a common center, from which any weak point can be strengthened and protected.

Source: *One Big Union of the Industrial Workers of the World*, 5th rev. ed. (Chicago: Industrial Workers of the World, 1957), pp. 16–17.

economic life of the entire country. The key word here is *administer.*

This is the same thing as Engels' statement that in the final stage of communism, the government of men will change to the administration of things. People will no longer be governed.

They will be free from government, but they will participate in administering the economic life of the country. The contention is that there need be no such thing as a political decision. The administration of things should be, according to anarcho-syndicalism, a fairly simple and mechanical operation which will not give rise to many conflicts that will have to be ironed out. When conflicts do arise because of the problems of allocating scarce goods, the workers, who are the people that most industries serve, will be in the best positions to know what is most important, what can be produced most inexpensively, and how to improve production. Therefore, these people should be making these decisions rather than the managers who are not in contact with the actual work. The anarcho-syndicalist also argues that putting the workers in control of the job will enable them to produce more, thus lessening the problem of the allocation of scarce goods. The anarcho-syndicalist thus argues that workers' control acts as a greater incentive to work.

Some anarcho-syndicalists have argued that the basis for the new society is to be found in the organization of the present trade unions. However, modern anarcho-syndicalists view the trade unions as essentially conservative groups, particularly in the leadership, that are directly opposed to any possiblity of workers' control. Therefore, modern anarcho-syndicalists are often in opposition to the union movement and see the unions cooperating with management and government rather than opposing them for the benefit of the worker. Although the idea of syndicalism originated as part of the trade-union movement in France, it has in its form of anarcho-syndicalism moved away from the movement and tends today to be in opposition to it.

The differences between communist anarchism and anarcho-syndicalism are not great. Anarcho-syndicalism is more directly concerned with the organization of industrial society than is communist anarchism, but both of them arrive at fundamentally the same conclusions. Both of them accept the notion that the workers in a given area should control the operation of that area, whether it be a commune as in communist anarchism or an industry as in anarcho-syndicalism, for the benefit of the society as a whole. It is assumed in both cases that the entire population will be workers, at least to the extent that they will be participating to some degree in the economic life of the society. Both of them believe that by removing coercion a viable society can operate. The difference is primarily found in the emphasis of anarcho-syndicalism on the operation of the industrial system.

Anarcho-syndicalism and communist anarchism developed a secondary level of organization that is important for understanding the course of anarchist thought. Both types of anarchism stress the need for some way of developing cooperation among communes or industries as well as within the individual commune or industry. Although the focus of most studies of anarchist thought has been on the individual and his freedom gained through the destruction of coercion, the anarchists have always argued that it is not possible to stop there. Except for the individualist anarchists, who will be discussed shortly, the primary focus of anarchism does not rest on the isolated individual. The focus of anarchism is on an individual within a noncoercive society. The emphasis is on producing the type of society that will allow the individual to be free. Most anarchists recognize that the small commune or industry is not sufficient for individuals in contemporary society. They have recognized that some cooperation is necessary among communes and industries in order to produce sufficient goods in sufficient diversity for each individual.

This is most clearly recognized in anarcho-syndicalism because its basic form of organization, the industry, is specialized. Therefore, in order to give each individual the goods that are necessary for life, there must be a high degree of cooperation among the industries to provide an efficient distribution system for the goods produced by the individual industries. Again, it is argued that the only way to handle this is through cooperation on the part of the workers within the various industries. To some extent it could be argued that what is looked for here is simply a form of enlightened self-interest, because each individual worker in a particular industry needs the products of a wide variety of industries. Therefore, in order to achieve this the individual workers will cooperate with workers from a wide variety of industries, because they all need the products of each and every industry. The anarcho-syndicalists believe that this cooperation can be developed readily once coercion disappears. This conviction is held, it seems, primarily because it is believed that such cooperation will be to the advantage of all the individuals within the society.

In order to do this all coercion must be abolished. This means government and, for the collectivist anarchist, capitalism must go. This, of course, raises the question of violence. Anarchists believe that no established authority will simply give up without a fight; therefore, violent revolution is likely to be the means to change.[11] The abolition of capitalism is a central concern of most anarchists because they see the workers exploited by the capitalist in about the same ways that Marx did. They thus argue for common ownership of the means of production and the distribution of goods according to need. Anarcho-capitalists, whom we will discuss shortly, believe that this system would exploit the best workers. The collectivist anarchists respond that capitalism exploits all the workers. It may be that this disagreement is incapable of being solved, but to put it in perspective, let us look at the individualist position.

INDIVIDUALIST ANARCHISM

The individualist anarchists recognize nothing above his ego and rebels against all discipline and all authority, divine or human. He accepts no morality and when he gives himself to the feelings of love, friendship, or sociability, he does so because it is a personal need, an egoistic satisfaction—because it pleases him to do it.[12]

Individualist anarchism is traditionally associated with Max Stirner. Essentially the position is as stated above; individuals

---

[11] For the controversy see the following: *Anarchism and Outrage* (London: Freedom Press, 1909); N[icolas] W[alter], "Anarchism, Bombs, And all That," *Freedom*, vol. 32 (January 23, 1971), pp. 1–2; Emile Armand (pseud.), "Reflections on Non-Violence," *Freedom*, vol. 23 (March 10, 1962), p. 4; Geoffrey Barfoot, "Anarchism and Violence," *Freedom*, vol. 29 (October 26, 1968), p. 4; Antony Fleming, "Anarchism and Revolution," *Anarchy 106*, vol. 9 (December 1969), pp 360–76; "Pacifism, Non-Violence and Anarchism," *Freedom*, vol. 23 (July 7, 1962), p. 3; Elisée Reclus, *Evolution and Revolution*, 7th ed. (London: W. Reeves, n.d.); Ronald Simpson, *The Anarchist Basis of Pacifism* (London: Stuart Morris Memorial Fund, Peace Pledge Union, n.d.; Lyman Tower Sargent, "Revolution, Evolution and Reform," *Anarchy 114*, vol. 10 (August 1970), pp. 253–57; and Jeremy Westall, "Anarchism and Violence," *Freedom*, vol. 24 (July 20, 1963), pp. 2, 4.

[12] Enzo Martucci, "Individualist Amoralism," *Minus One*, no. 16 (November/December 1966), p. 5. Trans. J.-P. S. from *L'Unique*, no. 37.

determine for themselves, out of their own needs and desires, what is right for them. Stirner even applies this to murder.[13]

Individualist anarchists do not completely reject cooperation between people. They argue that cooperation is essential for the fulfillment of some needs. But they contend that only the individualist, the true individualist of their own definition, is capable of genuinely forming a voluntary association with others. In addition, they never see this association as an end in itself but merely as a useful form for a temporary purpose. It must be the servant of the members, not dominate the members.

The individualist anarchist argues against the collective ownership of goods but is not convinced that the capitalist system is any better. Here one finds a major split in the ranks of individualist anarchists—on the one hand, there are those such as S. E. Parker who reject both capitalism and socialism and argue that they are not yet convinced that either system is valid within an individualist anarchist environment. In a review of this section of the first edition of this book, he says, "I do tend to believe these days that there is far more hope of a consistent individualism emerging from the 'free market' approach than from the 'free-communist' approach, most of whose advocates are heavily sold on collectivism."[14] On the other hand, there are the anarcho-capitalists who contend that the only form of economic life compatible with individualism is capitalism. Usually their approach is connected with a view of life similar to that of the Social Darwinist. They see life as a struggle for survival among men and hold that a socialist economic system supports those who do not deserve to survive.[15] Anarcho-capitalists take the position that all essential social services can be better operated privately for profit than by any government or commune, including the police, education, the military, and so forth.

Recently anarcho-capitalism has become a major area of

---

[13] See Max Stirner (pseud.), The Ego and His Own; The Case of the Individual against Authority, trans. Steven T. Byington, and ed. James J. Martin (New York: Libertarian Book Club, 1963), p. 190.

[14] S. E. Parker, "Review of Contemporary Political Ideologies; A Comparative Analysis," Minus One, no. 25 (December 1969), p. 11.

[15] Anarcho-capitalism seems to have developed out of what is now called libertarianism rather than anarchism. Libertarianism is the argument that some minimal government will continue to be necessary. See Jerome Tuccille, It Usually Begins with Ayn Rand (New York: Stein & Day, 1971).

concern in American social thought. This has been largely as a result of the publication of *Anarchy, State, and Utopia* by Robert Nozick which provides the most thorough defense of the position yet attempted. Nozick's concerns are no different from previous writers in the anarcho-capitalist tradition, but he has presented them in a more consistent and sophisticated manner and has thus attracted more response, and response from different circles, than had earlier writers. In addition, the establishment of the Libertarian party to promote the anarcho-capitalist perspective and to run candidates in elections has brought the position to a larger audience than had been previously aware of it. And clearly it has struck a sympathetic note among Americans.[16]

All of anarchism, whether communist, anarcho-syndicalist, or individualist, is concerned with the freedom of the individual. Anarchism is a system of thought that rejects control by any group but particularly by the organized group we call the state or the government. Anarchists argue that people are capable of freedom and that they are capable of cooperating together in voluntary association. They believe that human beings are willing and able to help each other. They believe that the human's best instincts are destroyed by the present organization of society. They feel, as did Marx, that true love between individuals is impossible, or at least difficult, under contemporary conditions. They feel that a morality system that rejects physical relationships without the sanction of church and state destroys the possibility of developing what Marx called the love-sex relationship. The anarchist does not insist upon or reject the simple monogamous marriage relationship. Individuals, they contend, must decide on what sort of relationship they want to live in. It is their life, and they must be free to make these decisions.

The anarchist also contends that there is a real responsibility

---

[16] On anarcho-capitalism, see Murray Rothbard, *America's Great Depression,* 2d ed. (Los Angeles: Nash Publishers, 1972); Rothbard, *For a New Liberty* (New York: Macmillan, 1973); Rothbard, *Man, Economy, and State,* 2 vols. (Los Angeles: Nash Publishers, 1970); and Rothbard, *Power and Market* (Menlo Park, Cal.: Institute for Humane Studies, 1970). See also Jerome Tuccille, *Radical Libertarianism; A Right Wing Alternative* (Indianapolis: Bobbs-Merrill, 1970); and Robert Nozick, *Anarchy, State, and Utopia* (New York: Basic Books, 1974).

on the part of parents in such a relationship to ensure freedom for their children. They feel that the contemporary educational system is destructive of freedom and creativity and any possibility of learning. They believe that there must be some type of educational system that is directed to the individual child, whatever his or her needs may be. This cannot be found, they contend, in the highly organized, overly complex educational system that we have today. It can be found in the small group that is concerned with educating for freedom; that does not convince itself that education is the ingestion of a myriad of facts that may not be relevant to the particular child's interest. They believe that a child given the freedom to choose and select and given the encouragement to follow his or her own bent will gradually find distinct interests and, getting interested, will apply the tremendous energies that children can develop to a study, an understanding, and a learning of those interests.

Much of what we are taught in our schools, the anarchist believes, is totally irrelevant to our lives; we waste many years in attempting to learn things that we will really never be interested in. A child should be encouraged to look at the world and interpret it on his or her own rather than being given answers. This approach to education puts a tremendous burden on the parent and the teacher. The teacher must develop a close relationship with the child in order to be able to understand the child's changing interests and to suggest to the child ways in which he or she might best fulfill current interests. This must be done without directing the child too much. The parent also must be capable of giving the child freedom. The parent must not control the child too much. Anarchist theories of child rearing and education have been some of the most innovative, instructive, and successful of any of the anarchist approaches to contemporary life.[17]

There is no proscription or support of religion. There is within anarchist circles considerable debate over the question of religious affiliation. Many argue that this is incompatible with

---

[17] See, for example, Herbert Read, *The Education of Free Men* (London: Freedom Press, 1944); A. S. Neill, *Summerhill; A Radical Approach to Child Rearing* (New York: Hart Publication Co., 1960); Ivan D. Illich, *Deschooling Society* (London: Calders & Boyars, 1971); and Peter Buckman, ed., *Education without Schools* (London: Souvenir Press, 1973).

anarchism, whereas others argue that it depends on the type of organization or church.

Still others, including the Catholic anarchists, such as Dorothy Day and Ammon Hennacy, who left the church shortly before he died, argue that faith in the doctrines of the church do not affect them as anarchists—that the church only speaks on matters of faith and morals; that it does not deal with the rest of their lives. Outside of these areas the Catholic anarchist considers himself to be completely free from the church. The catholic anarchist is merely a special case of contemporary anarchism. The individuals such as Dorothy Day and, for a time, Ammon Hennacy, who accept a highly authoritarian religion and at the same time consider themselves anarchists, are merely taking one part of their life, that part that deals with questions of religious faith, and accepting the dictates of the church. This faith, as long as it is restricted to religious questions and perhaps also moral questions, does not necessarily affect the social and political positions of the anarchist. It obviously could affect these positions in relationship to questions of morals, but this would depend on the individual's own temperament. Thus, the emphasis of anarchism is on voluntary association of individuals in a variety of forms, one of which is the commune.[18]

Anarchism will probably always remain a minor ideology. It is unlikely that anarchism will ever succeed in this world, but anarchism is essentially a humanistic belief in man. Anarchism is the ideology that has the most faith in man. It believes as no other ideology does that man is capable of freedom and cooperation.

CURRENT TRENDS

In the last few years there have been three developments that must be noted. First there has been the resurgence of anarchocapitalism discussed above. Second, there has been the discov-

[18] See, for example, W. David Wills, *Throw Away Thy Rod; Living with Difficult Children* (London: Victor Gollancz, 1960); Wills, *The Barns Experiment* (London: George Allen and Unwin, 1945); Alex Comfort; *Delinquency* (London: Freedom Press, 1951); John Hewetson, *Ill-Health, Poverty and the State* (London: Freedom Press, 1946); George Woodcock, *New Life to the Land* (London: Freedom Press, 1942); and Woodcock, *Railways and Society* (London: Freedom Press, 1943).

ery of various forms of anarchism by popular writers, particularly writers of science fiction. The most noteworthy of these writers are Poul Anderson, who has written many works from the perspective of anarcho-capitalism, and Ursula K. Le Guin, who has written a novel, *The Dispossessed, An Ambiguous Utopia* (1974), that depicts in detail and with sympathy the struggles of a successful anarchist society to hold true to its principles.

Finally, there is a controversy among anarchists. The argument is over whether or not a new anarchism developed in the 1960s was essentially different from anarchism as it has previously existed.[19] The supposed differences are great and cannot be gone into here in detail. Some of the differences relate to the social composition, age, class background, and the likes of the "new" as opposed to the "old" anarchism. Other differences relate to questions of tactics, such as violence versus nonviolence, that have always been controversial.

While a survey of the literature of the "new" anarchism[20] reveals significant stylistic differences, it is at least debatable whether or not there are significant differences in content. In most cases analysis shows that such differences do not exist, but at the same time there is an emphasis on spontaneity and a rejection of reasoned argument in the "new" anarchism that does not appear in the "old" anarchism.[21]

---

[19] The most explicit case of the controversy can be found in the differences between the first and second series of the British Journal *Anarchy*.

[20] The following give an idea of the approaches. Most important is Guy Debord, *La societe du spectacle* (Paris: Buchet-Chastel, 1971; unauthorized translation, Detroit: Black & Red, 1973). See also *Anarchy*, 2d series, and *Broadsheet* (Sydney Libertarians) for different examples of the periodical literature. In addition, see Christopher Gray, ed. and trans., *The Incomplete Work of the Situationist International* (London: Free Fall Publications, 1974); Rudolf de Jong, *Provos and Kabouters* (Buffalo, N.Y.: Friends of Malatesta, n.d.); *Hip Culture* (New York: Times Change Press, 1970); Jeff Nuttall, *Bomb Culture* (London: Paladin, 1968); Peter Stansill and David Zane Mairowitz, eds. *Bamn* (Harmondsworth: Penguin, 1971); *Surrealism and Revolution* (London: Wooden Shoe, n.d.); Roel Van Duyn, *Message of a Wise Kabouter*, trans. Hubert Hoskins (London: Duckworth, 1969); Raoul Vaneigem, *The Revolution of Everyday Life*, trans. John Fullerton and Paul Sieveking (London: Practical Paradise Publications, 1975); and *The Veritable Split in the International* (London: Harpo Press, 1974).

[21] The most sustained rejection of the thesis that there is a "new" anarchism can be found in N[icolas] W[alter], "Has Anarchism Changed?" *Freedom's Anarchist Review*, vol. 37 (April 17, May 1, June 26, July 10, 1976), pp. 9–10, 11–12, 9–10, 12–13.

SUGGESTED READINGS

Aldred, Guy. *Bakunin.* Glasgow: Strickland Press, 1940.

Arshinov, Peter. *History of the Makhnovist Movement (1918–1921).*
Trans. Lorraine Perlman and Fredy Perlman. Detroit: Black & Red
and Chicago: Solidarity, 1974.

Armand, E. *Anarchism and Individualism: Three Essays.* Trans. D.
T. W. London: S. E. Parker, n.d.

———. *What Individualist-Anarchists Want.* Trans. Mark William
Kramrisch. Adapted by S. E. Parker. London: S. E. Parker, n.d.

Avrich, Paul. *The Russian Anarchists.* Princeton, N.J.: Princeton University Press, 1967.

Bakunin, Mikhail. *Marxism, Freedom and the State.* Ed. and trans.
K. J. Kenafick. London: Freedom Press, 1950.

———. *God and the State.* New York: Dover Publications, 1970.

———. *Bakunin on Anarchy; Selected Works by the Activist-Founder
of World Anarchism.* Ed. and trans. Sam Dolgoff. New York: Alfred A. Knopf, 1971.

———. *Selected Writings.* Ed. Arthur Lehning. Trans. Steven Cox and
Olive Stevens. London: Jonethan Cape, 1973.

Baldelli, Giovanni. *Social Anarchism.* Chicago: Aldine–Atherton, 1971.

Barber, Benjamin. *Superman and Common Men; Freedom, Anarchy,
and the Revolution.* New York: Praeger, 1971.

Barrett, George (pseud. George Powell Ballard). *The First Person.*
London: Freedom Press, 1963.

Berkman, Alexander. *ABC of Anarchism.* 3d ed. London: Freedom
Press, 1964.

Berneri, C. *Peter Kropotkin; His Federalist Ideas.* London: Freedom
Press, 1942.

Bookchin, Murray (pseud.) *Post-Scarcity Anarchism.* Berkeley, Calif.:
Ramparts Press, 1971.

Bose, Atindranath. *A History of Anarchism.* Calcutta: World Press
Private Ltd., 1967.

Brailsford, H. N. *Shelley, Godwin, and Their Circle.* New York: Henry
Holt & Co., n.d.

Carr, E. G. *Michael Bakunin.* New York: Vintage Books, 1937.

Carter, April. *The Political Theory of Anarchism.* London: Routledge
& Kegan Paul, 1971.

Christie, Stuart, and Meltzer, Albert. *The Floodgates of Anarchy.* London: Kahn & Averill, 1970.

de Cleyre, Voltairine. *Selected Works of Voltairine de Cleyre.* Ed.
Alexander Berkman. New York: Mother Earth Publishing Co.,
1914.

Deleon, David. "The American as Anarchist: Social Criticism in the 1960s," *American Quarterly*, 25 (December 1973), pp. 516–37.

De Lubac, Henri, S.J. *The Un-Marxian Socialist: A Study of Proudhon*. Trans. R. E. Scantlebury. New York: Sheed & Ward, 1948.

Dolgoff, Sam, ed. *The Anarchist Collectives; Workers' Self-management in the Spanish Revolution 1936–1939*. New York: Free Life Editions, 1974.

Eltzbacher, Paul. *Anarchism; Exponents of the Anarchist Philosophy*. Trans. Steven T. Byington. Ed. James J. Martin. London: Freedom Press, 1960.

Godwin, William. *Enquiry Concerning Political Justice and Its Influence on Morals and Happiness*. Ed. F. E. L. Priestley. 3 vols. Toronto: University of Toronto Press, 1946.

Goldman, Emma. *Anarchism and Other Essays*. New York: Dover Publications, 1970.

———. *Living My Life*. 2 vols. New York: Dover Publications, 1970.

Goodman, Paul, ed. *Seeds of Liberation*. New York: George Braziller, 1964.

Guérin, Daniel. *Anarchism from Theory to Practice*. Trans. Mary Klopper. New York: Monthly Review Press, 1970.

Hennacy, Ammon. *The Book of Ammon*. The author, 1965.

———. *The One-Man Revolution in America*. Salt Lake City: Ammon Hennacy Publications, 1970.

Hoffman, Robert L. *Revolutionary Justice; The Social and Political Theory of P.-J. Proudhon*. Urbana, Ill.: University of Illinois Press, 1972.

Illich, Ivan. *Deschooling Society*. New York: Harper & Row, 1971.

Jacker, Corinne. *The Black Flag of Anarchy; Antistatism in the United States*. New York: Charles Scribner's Sons, 1968.

Joll, James. *The Anarchists*. London: Eyre & Spottiswoode, 1964.

Kornbluth, Joyce L., ed. *Rebel Voices; An I.W.W. Anthology*. Ann Arbor, Mich.: University of Michigan Press, 1968.

Krimerman, Leonard I., and Perry, Lewis, eds. *Patterns of Anarchy: A Collection of Writings on the Anarchist Tradition*. Garden City, N.Y.: Doubleday & Co., 1966.

Kropotkin, Peter. *The Conquest of Bread*. New York: G. P. Putnam's Sons, 1907.

———. *The Great French Revolution 1789–1793*. 2 vols. Trans. N. F. Dryhurst. New York: Vanguard Press, 1909.

———. *Ethics: Origin and Development*. Trans. Louis S. Friedland and Joseph R. Piroshnikoff. New York: Tudor Publishing Co., 1924.

———. *Mutual Aid; A Factor of Evolution*. Boston: Extending Horizons Books, 1955.

CONTEMPORARY POLITICAL IDEOLOGIES

————. *Memoirs of a Revolutionist.* Ed. James Allen Rogers. Garden City, N.Y.: Doubleday & Co., 1962.

————. *Fields, Factories and Workshops.* New York: Benjamin Blom, 1968.

————. *Fields, Factories and Workshops Tomorrow.* Ed. Colin Ward. London: George Allen & Unwin, 1974.

————. *The Essential Kropotkin.* Ed. Emile Caposeya and Keitha Tompkins. New York: Liveright, 1975.

————. *Kropotkin's Revolutionary Pamphlets.* Ed. Roger N. Baldwin. New York: Dover Publications, 1970.

————. *Selected Writings on Anarchism and Revolution.* Ed. Martin A. Miller. Cambridge, Mass.: M.I.T. Press, 1970.

Malatesta, Errico. *Anarchy.* 8th ed. London: Freedom Press, 1949.

Martin, James J. *Men against the State: The Expositors of Individualist Anarchism in America, 1827–1908.* Colorado Springs, Colo.: Ralph Myles, 1970.

Morris, William. *News from Nowhere or An Epoch of Rest; Being Some Chapters from a Utopian Romance.* Chicago: Charles H. Kerr, n.d.

Nettlau, M. *Bibliographie de l'anarchie.* New York: Burt Franklin, 1968.

Ni Dieu ni maitre. *Anthologie historique du mouvement anarchiste.* Paris: Editions de Delphes, 1965.

Nozick, Robert. *Anarchy, State, and Utopia.* New York: Basic Books, 1974.

Parker, S. E. *Individualist Anarchism: An Outline.* London: S. E. Parker, 1965.

Peters, Victor. *Nestor Makhno; The Life of an Anarchist.* Winnipeg: Echo Books, 1970.

Proudhon, Pierre-Joseph. *General Idea of the Revolution in the Nineteenth Century.* Trans. John Beverley Robinson. London: Freedom Press, 1923.

————. *Oeuvres choisies.* Paris: Gallimard, 1967.

————. *Selected Writings of P.-J. Proudhon.* Ed. Stewart Edwards, and trans. Elizabeth Fraser. Garden City, N.Y.: Anchor Books, 1969.

————. *What Is Property: An Inquiry into the Principle of Right and of Government.* Two volumes in one. Trans. Benjamin R. Tucker. London: William Reeves, n.d.

Read, Herbert. *The Philosophy of Anarchism.* London: Freedom Press, 1940.

————. *The Education of Free Men.* London: Freedom Press, 1944.

————. *Poetry and Anarchism.* 2d ed. London: Freedom Press, 1947.

————. *Anarchy and Order; Essays in Politics.* London: Faber & Faber, 1954.

Richards, Vernon, comp. and ed.   *Errico Malatesta; His Life and Ideas.* London: Freedom Press, 1965.

Rocker, Rudolf.   *Nationalism and Culture.* Trans. Ray E. Chase. Los Angeles: Rocker Publications Committee, 1937.

Schweitzer, Jean-Pierre.   *O Idios; Three Essays on Individualist Anarchism.* London: S. E. Parker, 1966.

Spring, Joel.   *A Primer of Libertarian Education.* New York: Free Life Editions, 1975.

Stirner, Max (pseud.).   *The Ego and His Own: The Case of the Individual against Authority.* Trans. Steven T. Byington, and ed. James M. Martin. New York: Libertarian Book Club, 1963.

———.   *The False Principle of Our Education or Humanism and Realism.* Trans. Robert H. Beebe. Ed. James J. Martin. Colorado Springs, Colo.: Ralph Myles, 1967.

Taylor, Michael.   *Anarchy and Cooperation.* New York: John Wiley & Sons, 1976.

Thomas, Joan.   *The Years of Grief and Laughter. A 'Biography' of Ammon Hennacy.* Phoenix: Hennacy Press, 1974.

Tolstoy, Leo.   *The Law of Love and the Law of Violence.* Trans. Mary Koutouzow Tolstoy. London: Anthony Blond, 1970.

Tucker, Benjamin R.   *Individual Liberty; Selections from the Writings of Benjamin R. Tucker.* Ed. C. L. S. New York: Vanguard Press, 1926.

Tullock, Gordon, ed.   *Explorations in the Theory of Anarchy.* Blacksburg, Va.: Center for the Study of Public Choice, Virginia Polytechnic Institute and State University, 1972.

Ward, Colin.   *Anarchy in Action.* London: George Allen & Unwin, 1973.

———.   *Housing; An Anarchist Approach.* London: Freedom Press, 1976.

Woodcock, George.   *Anarchy or Chaos.* London: Freedom Press, 1944.

———.   *William Godwin: A Biographical Study.* London: Porcupine Press, 1946.

———.   *The Writer and Politics.* London: Porcupine Press, 1948.

———.   *Pierre-Joseph Proudhon: A Biography.* London: Routledge & Kegan Paul, 1956.

———.   *Anarchism; A History of Libertarian Ideas and Movements.* Cleveland, Ohio: World Publishing Co., 1962.

———, and Avakumovic, Ivan.   *The Anarchist Prince; A Biographical Study of Peter Kropotkin.* London: T. V. Broadman, 1950.

Woolf, Robert Paul.   *In Defense of Anarchism.* New York: Harper & Row, 1970.

7

The New Left

Although significantly less important than in the 1960s and early 1970s, the New Left[1] is still important. It had a great impact on the thinking of an entire generation, the one now in its late twenties and early thirties. It will continue to have a growing influence in most Western democracies. The New Left is also closely linked to both anarchism and to the ideologies of the Third World. This shows that certain aspects of contemporary radical ideologies are held in common by divergent groups. In addition, two movements closely linked to the New Left, the black movement and the women's movement, clearly will be of continuing significance in a variety of countries. Finally, some of the terrorism that is evident around the world is linked to certain elements of the New Left.

The term, *New Left,* was first used by a group of liberal Marxists centered around the *New Left Review* in 1959. The term was then appropriated by the growing world student movement and the mass media in the mid-1960s.[2] It is now used to cover a wide variety of movements and individuals.

There are three reasonable approaches to a study of the New

[1] For a more extensive and detailed analysis of New Left thought, see Lyman Tower Sargent, *New Left Thought: An Introduction* (Homewood, Ill.: Dorsey Press, 1972).

[2] For chronologies of the movement, see Julian Nagel, ed., *Student Power* (London: Merlin Press, 1969), pp. 225–35, and Massimo Teodori, ed., *The New Left: A Documentary History* (Indianapolis, Ind.: Bobbs-Merrill Co., 1969), pp. 447–82.

Left. One could do a study of the history of the movement,[3] an analysis of the organizations involved in the movement, or an analysis of the ideas that tie the movement together. I have chosen to take the third approach primarily because it is my contention that the ideas are the defining characteristics of the New Left and that the movement cannot be understood from any other perspective.

Among the groups that compose the movement, including the black groups and the women's groups, there are widely divergent emphases, but all agree on the goals I set forth with the exception of the purely reformist groups. All the radical groups clearly agree on these points. The major disagreements within the New Left are over tactics and to discuss these points in detail is beyond the scope of this chapter. It should be kept in mind, therefore, that the focus is on the general agreements, and it should be remembered that disagreements are plentiful.

In looking at the New Left we shall look first at the New Left's criticism of contemporary society and then at the New Left's values and goals. Then, we shall look at the New Left utopia by way of conclusion.

CRITICISM OF CONTEMPORARY SOCIETY

Throughout most of its life, the New Left has been noted for its critical stance toward contemporary society rather than its goals. In order to fully understand the impact and the importance of the New Left we must note its attack on contemporary Western culture.

The most basic criticism that the New Left made was hypocrisy—the divergence between word and deed. This point is not monopolized by the New Left; it is widely believed that the expressed values of Western society must not be deeply felt because so few attempts seem to be made to actually practice them.

In addition to this basic criticism, there are so many points of attack that I shall simply list them in brief notes.

---

[3] See Edward J. Bacciocco, Jr., *The New Left in America; Reform to Revolution 1956 to 1970* (Stanford, Calif.: Hoover Institution Press, 1974); Kirkpatrick Sale, *SDS* (New York: Vintage Books, 1973); and Irwin Unger, *The Movement: A History of the American New Left 1959–1972* (New York: Dodd, Mead, 1974).

I. The political system.
   A. Insufficient means included in representative democracy for the people to be involved in the decision-making process.
   B. Corruption.
   C. Resistance to significant change.
   D. Political repression.
II. The economic system.
   A. Poverty alongside great wealth.
   B. Emphasis on unnecessary consumer goods rather than socially beneficial production.
   C. Centralization of economic power—monopoly capitalism.
   D. Lack of concern with side effects of the industrial process, such as pollution.
   E. Economic imperialism (neocolonialism)—exploitation of developing nations.
III. Racism and sexism.
   Discrimination against minority groups and women in all aspects of life.
IV. Socialization system.
   A. Education.
      1. Lack of "relevance."
      2. Authoritarian atmosphere.
   B. Religion.
      1. Not "relevant."
      2. Tied to the capitalist system.
      3. Particular target of the charge of hypocrisy.
   C. Family.
      1. Marriage an institution of private property.
      2. Marriage should not need religious and/or legal approval.
      3. Hypocrisy about sex—sexual repression.
      4. Poor way to raise children.

THE BASIC VALUES AND GOALS

It is possible to analyze the New Left through a series of values and goals that seem to be found among all the groups and individuals that make up the movement. These are:

1. The emphasis on action.
2. The search for the authentic self.
3. Community.
4. Equality.
5. Liberty.
6. Participatory democracy.
7. Revolution.

1. *Action.*   Probably the most basic assumption of the New Left, drawn in large part from the French existentialists, is that action is more important than thought. This means (1) that individuals define themselves and their values through their deeds rather than their words; (2) that change cannot or will not be brought about by the pen; and (3) that there is a degree of distrust and dislike of the intellectual on the New Left. This principle incorporates, more for the New Left than it did for the existentialists, a basic antiintellectualism. This antiintellectualism, in addition to being an American tradition, also relates to the basic criticism of Western society—hypocrisy. The divergence between expressed values and the actions based on these values coupled with a predilection for action tends toward an emphasis on the immediate, spontaneous act and a disparagement of reasoned discourse.

Since it is exceedingly difficult to express feelings precisely in words, the New Left has searched for other means of communication. The art forms of the 1960s, happenings, the environments directed at one or a combination of the senses, are attempts to get beyond the verbal to a more total communication. Earlier, in the 1950s, poets such as Allen Ginsberg tried to shake and jolt people out of their lethargy and their preconceptions. With obscenities and with the language molded to meet new thought patterns, these writers were beginning to do the same thing that later shifted from the verbal and became the happenings. The same point can be made about the music. Although the words often express the sentiments of the New Left, they are much less important than the total environment produced by the sound.[4]

---

[4] For a general discussion of the relationship between the New Left and art, see Donald Drew Egbert, *Social Radicalism and the Arts; Western Europe* (New York: Alfred A. Knopf, 1970), pp. 359–64, 571–80, and passim.

2. *The authentic self.* Although most intellectuals dispar-
age the short movement called the beatniks, they are important
for understanding the development of New Left thought. In the
first place, a number of individuals, such as Ginsberg and Gary
Snyder, figure prominently in both cultures. Second, the criticisms of contemporary society are strikingly similar. Third, the
basic motivation of the beats (coming from the word *beatific*)
was the same as a strong current now found on the New Left—
a desperate search for something authentic, something solid in
the self. Clearly this was transmitted from the existentialists, but
it was transmitted through the beat subculture.

Probably the greatest difference between the beats and the
New Left is that the New Left has some hope of finding something. The beats were called the product of the age of apathy—
they were in reality the generation of despair. The primary beat
novels, *On the Road* (1957) and *The Dharma Bums* (1958) by
Jack Kerouac, are pervaded by a sense of despair periodically
broken by a glory in being alive.

The New Left is still searching for this authentic self, and it
seems to have some hope of finding it in notions of community, the group, and, of course, action. Often the last idea is expressed in the concept of revolution. Hence a number of the
basic goals and values of the New Left are tied together with
the search for the authentic self.[5] This is particularly true of the
concept of community.

3. *Community.* Notions of community or group consciousness are not common or particularly popular in American
political thought, but they form the central concept in New Left
thought. The basic idea is most often associated with the hippie communes, but it is a pervasive motif of the New Left. The
revolutionary moves from communal apartment to communal
apartment; the typical hippie lives in a rural or urban community withdrawn from the surrounding straight world.[6]

---

[5] This may account for the popularity of the novels of Herman Hesse, particularly *Magister Ludi,* also called *The Bead Game* and *Das Glasperlenspiel*
(1943), which presents a search for an undefined goal certainly related to the
self through both individual and community effort.

[6] See Gary Snyder, "Why Tribe," in *Earth House Hold,* reprinted in Harold
Jaffe and John Tytell, eds., *The American Experience; A Radical Reader* (New
York: Harper & Row, 1970), pp. 258–61.

The emphasis on community, particularly in the new communal movement, makes the connection with the ideals of communal socialism clear. The notion here is essentially the same, the extended family as ideal. This does not simply mean sharing money. It is a familylike atmosphere where all contribute and all are free, within the limits of the available resources, to take as they need, fairly and with consideration for the others. This is possible due to the mutually supportive atmosphere of the community.

The new community has a wide variety of sexual relations, and this must be stressed because it is felt to be important by most of the New Left. One of the main targets of the charge of hypocrisy has of course been the attitudes toward sex in contemporary society. And although most sexual relations in the communes are monogamous and heterosexual, albeit often of short duration, all other types of sexual relations are found and accepted—group sex, lesbianism, male homosexuality, bisexuality. Obviously this point relates closely to liberty, but it is the supportive, accepting atmosphere of the small community that makes it possible.

The hippie commune is the best known form of the community, and although the commune movement has probably reached its peak, at least for the present, many thousands of people tried a new lifestyle and many are still living one.[7] This emphasis on community which is common to all modern radicals is one of the most interesting contemporary developments, but it is much too early to say what it means.[8]

4. *Equality.* Since in the United States the New Left developed out of the civil rights movement, it is not surprising that considerations of equality have provided a significant area of concern in New Left thought. The New Left is traditionally

---

[7] The new communalism has produced a rash of studies. The best general studies so far are: Richard Fairfield, *Communes USA; A Personal Tour* (Baltimore: Penguin Books, 1972); Rosabeth Moss Kanter, *Commitment and Community; Communes and Utopias in Sociological Perspective* (Cambridge, Mass.: Harvard University Press, 1972); Keith Melville, *Communes in the Counter Culture; Origins, Theories, Styles of Life* (New York: William Morrow & Co , 1972); and Laurence Veysey, *The Communal Experience; Anarchist and Mystical Counter-Cultures in America* (New York: Harper & Row, 1973).

[8] For two attempts to do so, see Charles A. Reich, *The Greening of America* (New York: Random House, 1970); and Philip E. Slater, *The Pursuit of Loneliness: American Culture at the Breaking Point* (Boston: Beacon Press, 1970).

democratic in its concern with political and legal equality, and these notions are reflections of the civil rights movement and its concern with reforming the system.

The New Left views economic equality as a singularly important mechanism for bringing about political and legal equality. The New Left is socialist in its orientation with the traditional democratic socialist concern with greatly diminishing the degree of economic inequality within society. The New Left has on the whole been unexceptional in its comments on economic questions and so has contributed little except vague comments about socialism.

Probably the most interesting of the New Left's developments in the area of equality has been in social equality. There seem to be two points involved here. First, there is the more or less traditional notion of equality—that individuals are to be treated the same in certain specifiable areas. The second, and much more interesting point, is that difference is to be recognized. The argument is a little difficult to specify, but it seems to focus on (1) a rejection of the notion that most differences are unimportant, (2) an assertion that certain differences have positive value, and (3) the contention that individuals must be accorded the same rights within society.

The importance of this conception of equality can be found in two areas. First, it is a departure from most democratic theory that asserts that differences are fairly unimportant. Second, it rejects the general practice that certain differences, such as sex and race, bring inferior status. The differences are seen as positive rather than negative, but it is stressed that treatment of individuals should be the same.

Of course the two best known movements related to the New Left, the black movement and the women's movement, stress this point. Both advocate and are working for a new concept of equality, one in which differences among people are accepted, even encouraged. But the key point is that these differences will no longer mean different treatment. Racial and sexual prejudices are deeply engrained in our society. Some progress has been made toward eliminating the most obvious forms of discrimination, but there is still much overt and covert discrimination and these movements will persist and, I am sure, continue to grow.

The relationship of this conception of equality to the idea of community should be fairly clear. First, groups that assert their difference provide one basis for the formation of community life. In this way, there might develop a community drawn from the black movement or some other group that has an established group identity. Second, within the community, individuals are treated equally. Each person shares the goods of the community as he or she needs them. They contribute on the same basis; as goods are acquired that are needed by the community, they are donated to the community.

5. *Liberty*. This is to be seen in conjunction with an emphasis on individual freedom. There is no compulsion to participate in the community. If individuals do not find the mores of one community congenial, they can try to find another that is more suitable.

The New Left is noted for slogans such as "Do your own thing," and the notion of liberty is important to the New Left. First, there is the general point that contemporary culture is considered too restrictive. Therefore, the New Left wants to remove the restrictions. Second, there is the assertion that everyone must be accorded certain basic economic rights. Again, this is seen primarily as a criticism of contemporary society's failure to provide the necessities of life to everyone. The New Left contends that society must be restructured to ensure that everyone has food, clothing, shelter, and whatever else is essential to life. Third, each person must in addition then be free to find and express his or her own personality in his or her own way. This entails the traditional democratic rights of free speech, assembly, press, and so forth.

It can, of course, be contended that members of the New Left do not always allow others the exercise of these freedoms. They have attempted to stop, and sometimes succeeded in stopping, their opponents from speaking. To some extent this may be seen as a tactical question, but that hides a deeper point. Some believe that any means are appropriate to bring about the goals, but the main point is that the opponent (1) excludes the New Left from a fair hearing by its manipulation of the media; and (2) is so conditioned by contemporary society that it cannot give the New Left a fair hearing. Therefore, (1) stopping speakers is simply using the tactics of the enemy, and (2) it is a device that may shock the opponent into examining his position.

In addition to free speech, and so on, the freedom to find and express one's authentic self means the ability to experiment with a variety of lifestyles, which in turn entails the freedom to do anything that does not harm another. One may harm oneself in any way one wishes. The only limit is harming another. This limit is obviously modified during a revolution.

Finally, the individual and society are seen as freeing themselves from a dependence on material goods. There is an ethos of voluntary poverty on the New Left. This is true first to identify with the oppressed masses, but second, and more importantly, it is a step toward freeing society from the oppression of consumerism.

6. *Participatory democracy.* It appears that participatory democracy is a device by which direct democracy might be feasible within a large society. Essentially participatory democracy suggests that, instead of having a large representative body, the decision-making structure be significantly altered so that there would be many small decision-making bodies throughout any given area. There have been very few statements about the level of government or administration above this small local unit. Thus there seems to be little thought of mechanisms for overcoming the probably inevitable conflict between groups who perceive the effect on their lives of a particular decision to be significantly different. Thus there seems to be no way of reconciling the interests of two groups who differ on a particular question. There is some notion that power should reside with those who are most directly affected by a particular decision, but the objections to this are so obvious that it cannot be thought of without major revision and refinement. In this context it may be worthwhile to state the most obvious of these objections—the impossibility in most cases of measuring direct effect.

On the other hand, although participatory democracy is vague, we must not ignore the role it plays in New Left thought. Participatory democracy is the logical extension of the ideas of community and social equality mentioned above. No matter which notion came first in time, participatory democracy would only be possible if the other two conditions were met. Whether or not it would be possible even under those conditions is another problem.

7. *Revolution.* The New Left believes that it will take a revolution to change contemporary Western society. At one time the revolution was to be peaceful and nonviolent and take place through gradual reform. More and more it has become violent and bloody. The change is due to two main factors—frustration and the idealization of the guerrilla fighter. Clearly frustration is the primary reason, but if the guerrilla fighter images of Mao, Ho, and particularly Che were not available the frustration might have taken different directions.

The New Left is frustrated by the unwillingness of Western society to respond positively to its criticism, criticism that is so obviously correct. Hence, the shift began to take place to a belief that Western society has gone so far it cannot be reformed from within but must be toppled and a new, better society built in its place.

The revolution plays a peculiar role in New Left thought. First, it is a necessary step before the new society can come about. Second, it is seen as taking place over a long period of time, and it has already begun. Therefore, some members of the New Left today consider themselves to be active revolutionaries. And the revolution justifies all. Society is so corrupt that it must be changed root and branch before a good society will be possible. The Symbionese Liberation Army (SLA) was a manifestation of this.

The New Left is split on this point. Many favor violent revolution. Many still believe in the efficacy of nonviolence. But all want the revolution. Currently, the most interesting development in New Left revolutionary thought is the rediscovery of Leon or Lev Trotsky, particularly his concept of the *permanent revolution,* although not really as he meant it. Trotsky developed his theory of the permanent revolution for specific situations in Russia about 1904.[9] One aspect of this specific argument is being applied by contemporary followers of Trotsky to the developing nations—the idea that it is not necessary to develop

---

[9] See Leon Trotsky, *What Is the Permanent Revolution? Three Concepts of the Russian Revolution* (Berkeley, Calif.: Pinetree Publications, 1965). Originally published 1942.

a fully capitalist state before communism is possible. Again this constant identification with the developing nations by parts of the New Left should be clearly noted.

But most of the New Left has picked up on the phrase "the permanent revolution" rather than Trotsky's specific meaning. It has become the notion, that while it is impossible to win a revolution in the West now, constant pressure can be kept on the system by underground groups such as the SLA and Weatherpeople. And this continuing revolution can win.

THE NEW LEFT UTOPIA

In a brief summary let us try to construct a model of the future society envisioned by the New Left—its utopia. Since a full description of the future society would be overly repetitious and consume too much space, I shall simply outline it.

Political system.
   Participatory democracy—town meeting or direct democracy made possible by the reorganization of society into small communities. Government primarily concerned with the administration of the economic system and ensuring that each individual has the basic necessities of life.
Economic system.
   Public ownership of all large industries, transportation, and so forth. Distribution on the basis of need wherever possible. Restructuring of the economic system to reduce the production of inessentials. Heavy reliance on automation combined with a growth of craft industries.
Social stratification and mobility systems—nonexistent.
Socialization system.
   Family.
      Marriage and sexual relations based on free choice without need of religious and/or legal sanction.
      Children raised by the community.
   Education.
      Material taught determined by students and teachers in free and equal consultation.
      All work desired to be made available.
Religion—based on free choice.

These are the basic characteristics of the future society of the New Left. Many details have been left out, but the important characteristics have been noted. As with any utopia, it is likely to be changed in practice.

CURRENT TRENDS

Most of the New Left have left the cause, which probably makes the remaining revolutionists more desperate and more violent. The New Left was a movement of hope. Banners proclaimed *Be realistic—Demand the impossible* and members of the New Left truly believed that what others proclaimed as impossible reforms were not only possible but within reach. The New Left was frustrated by its own inabilities and the slow response of government. But the generation of hope became a generation of despair and apathy only when shown to be correct in its criticism. Watergate demonstrated that so many of the points the New Left argued in their attack on contemporary American society were true and even the New Left was disillusioned by being proved correct. But, at the same time, there remains a remnant of hope and social concern in a large number of people.

Two groups that grew together with the New Left later split from it. The first of these, the black movement, gave rise to the New Left in the United States. It was the activities of black and white students in the South, particularly in the Student Non-Violent Coordinating Committee (SNCC), that radicalized a generation of students. But the blacks early learned that if they were to continue in the direction they wanted, they would have to insist that it was a black movement controlled by blacks and separate from the New Left.

While much of the New Left idealized poverty, blacks lived in it and found their white friends to be naive at best. In addition the development of a black consciousness, symbolized best by the slogan *Black Is Beautiful* began to teach an entire race that they had been robbed of their past and their culture. Thus many blacks identified with the emerging African countries and some of them saw blacks in the United States as a colonized country that must be freed.

All parts of the New Left forged links with revolutionary and nationalist movements around the world and with New Left groups, particularly in Europe. The abortive revolution in France in 1968, the unrest in the German and Italian universities and the continuing movements in Africa, Asia, and South America linked the New Left to a worldwide liberation movement. But in the United States the blacks learned that reform was having an effect and that most blacks were not supportive of either violence or an independent black nation within the United States.

But black liberation means something slightly different from national liberation, as does women's liberation. The emphasis is on the rediscovery of lost liberty, lost culture, and lost self. The emphasis is on the creation of new relationships within society rather than among countries. These new relationships fit the New Left model, if not the New Left practice, by emphasizing wholeness, independence, equality, and a community of the oppressed in solidarity against the oppressor.

The best exemplar of this is the women's movement, because it developed in large part as a result of hypocrisy within the New Left. Women activists came to see that they were expected to make coffee, type, and provide sex and to stay out of the way when the men were making decisions. The women became aware of their oppression and, failing to convince the men of the New Left and the black movement, split off and founded a new movement. And it is, of course, the women's movement that is having the greatest impact on American society. Women are insisting that they be treated as equals, that they be free to follow their own interests rather than being automatically assigned to socially stereotyped roles.

It is too early yet to assess the full impact of any of these movements, but it is clear that they have changed and are still changing the face of American life. And the women's movement in particular is just beginning to be felt in other countries. Perhaps even more significant change is yet to come.

SUGGESTED READINGS

An extensive bibliography will be found on pp. 169–84 of Sargent, Lyman Tower, *New Left Thought*. Therefore, I have simply updated that list here while still including the most important older works.

Adelson, Alan. *SDS; A Profile.* New York: Charles Scribner's Sons, 1972.

Bacciocco, Edward J., Jr., *The New Left in America; Reform to Revolution 1956–1970.* Stanford, Calif.: Hoover Institution Press, 1974.

Baran, Paul A., and Sweezy, Paul M. *Monopoly Capital; An Essay on the American Economic and Social Order.* New York: Monthly Review Press, 1966.

Brown, Bernard E. *Protest in Paris; Anatomy of a Revolt.* Morristown, N.J.: General Learning Press, 1974.

Carmichael, Stokely, and Hamilton, Charles V. *Black Power; The Politics of Liberation in America.* New York: Vintage Books, 1967.

Cleaver, Eldridge. *Soul on Ice.* New York: Dell Publishing Co., 1965.

Clutterbuck, Richard. *Protest and the Urban Guerrilla.* London: Cassell, 1973.

Cohn-Bendit, Daniel, and Cohn-Bendit, Gabriel. *Obsolete Communism; The Left-Wing Alternative.* Trans. Arnold Pomerana. London: Andre Deutsch, 1968.

Cook, Terrence E., and Morgan, Patrick M., eds. *Participatory Democracy.* San Francisco: Canfield Press, 1971.

Diamond, Stephen. *What the Trees Said; Life on a New Age Farm.* New York: Delacorte Press, 1971.

Ehrenreich, Barbara, and Ehrenreich, John E. *Long March, Short Spring; The Student Uprising at Home and Abroad.* New York: Monthly Review Press, 1969.

Fairfield, Richard. *Communes USA; A Personal Tour.* Baltimore: Penguin Books, 1972.

Fanon, Frantz. *The Wretched of the Earth.* Trans. Constance Farrington. New York: Grove Press, 1963.

Hayden, Tom. *Rebellion and Repression.* New York: Meridian Books, 1969.

————. *Trial.* New York: Holt, Rinehart & Winston, 1970.

Hoffman, Abbie (pseud. Free). *Revolution for the Hell of It.* New York: Dial Press, 1968.

————. *Steal This Book.* New York: Pirate Editions, 1971.

Houriet, Robert. *Getting Back Together.* New York: Coward, McCann & Geoghegan, 1971.

Jones, Beverley, and Brown, Judith. *Toward a Female Liberation Movement.* Boston: New England Free Press, n.d.

Kanter, Rosabeth Moss. *Commitment and Community; Communes and Utopias in Sociological Perspective.* Cambridge, Mass.: Harvard University Press, 1972.

Katz, Elia. *Armed Love.* New York: Holt, Rinehart & Winston, 1971.

Keniston, Kenneth. *Young Radicals: Notes on Committed Youth.* New York: Harcourt Brace Jovanovich, 1968.

Kerouac, Jack.   *On the Road*. New York: New American Library, 1957.

———.   *The Dharma Bums*. New York: New American Library, 1958.

Kinkade, Kathleen.   *A Walden Two Experiment; The First Five Years of Twin Oaks Community*. New York: William Morrow & Co., 1973.

Kolko, Gabriel.   *The Decline of American Radicalism in the Twentieth Century*. Boston: New England Free Press, n.d. Reprinted from *Studies on the Left*, September/October, 1966.

Kornbluth, Jesse, ed.   *Notes from the New Underground; An Anthology*. New York: Viking Press, 1968.

Kunen, James Simon.   *The Strawberry Statement: Notes of a College Revolutionary*. New York: Random House, 1968.

Lipset, Seymour Martin, and Altbach, Philip G., eds.   *Students in Revolt*. Boston: Houghton Mifflin, 1969. Also appeared as *Daedalus*, Winter 1968.

Long, Priscilla, ed.   *The New Left; A Collection of Essays*. Boston: Porter Sargent, 1969.

McAfee, Kathy, and Wood, Myrna.   *What Is the Revolutionary Potential of Women's Liberation?* Boston: New England Free Press, n.d. Better known under title *Bread and Roses*. Appeared originally in *Leviathan*, 1969.

Marcuse, Herbert.   *One Dimensional Man; Studies in the Ideology of Advanced Industrial Society*. Boston: Beacon Press, 1964.

———.   *An Essay on Liberation*. Boston: Beacon Press, 1969.

Melville, Keith.   *Communes in the Counter Culture; Origins, Theories, Styles of Life*. New York: William Morrow & Co., 1972.

Meyers, William, and Rinard, Park.   *Making Activism Work*. New York: Gordon and Breach, 1972.

Miles, Michael W.   *The Radical Probe; The Logic of Student Rebellion*. New York: Athenaeum, 1973.

Millett, Kate.   *Sexual Politics*. Garden City, N.Y.: Doubleday & Co., 1970.

Mills, Richard.   *Young Outsiders; A Study of Alternative Communities*. New York: Pantheon Books, 1973.

Morgan, Robin, ed.   *Sisterhood Is Powerful; An Anthology of Writings from the Women's Liberation Movement*. New York: Random House, 1970.

Oglesby, Carl, ed.   *The New Left Reader*. New York: Grove Press, 1969.

Roszak, Theodore.   *The Making of a Counter Culture; Reflections on the Technocratic Society and Its Youthful Opposition*. Garden City, N.Y.: Doubleday & Co., 1969.

Rothchild, John, and Susan Wolf.   *The Children of the Counterculture*. Garden City: Doubleday, 1976.

Rubin, Jerry. *Do It! Scenarios of the Revolution*. New York: Simon & Schuster, 1970.

Sale, Kirkpatrick. *SDS*. New York: Vintage Books, 1973.

Sargent, Lyman Tower. *New Left Thought: An Introduction*. Homewood, Ill.: Dorsey Press, 1972.

Tanner, Leslie B., ed. *Voices from Women's Liberation*. New York: New American Library, 1970.

Teodori, Massimo, ed. *The New Left: A Documentary History*. Indianapolis, Ind.: Bobbs-Merrill Co., 1969.

Trotsky, Leon. *Terrorism and Communism; A Reply to Karl Kautsky*. Ann Arbor, Mich.: University of Michigan Press, 1961.

————. *The New Course*. Ann Arbor, Mich.: University of Michigan Press, 1965.

Unger, Irwin. *The Movement: A History of the American New Left 1959–1972*. New York: Dodd, Mead, 1974.

Veysey, Laurence. *The Communal Experience; Anarchist and Mystical Counter-Cultures in America*. New York: Harper & Row, 1973.

Vickers, George R. *The Formation of the New Left; The Early Years*. Lexington, Mass.: Lexington Books, 1975.

Ware, Cellestine. *Woman Power; The Movement for Women's Liberation*. New York: Tower Publications, 1970.

Wood, James L. *New Left Ideology: Its Dimensions and Development*. Beverly Hills: Sage Publication, 1975.

Periodicals have been particularly important in the development of New Left thought. Below is a short list of some of the more important ones. Some no longer exist; others may go out of existence or appear any time.

Guardian (New Left from 1967 on.)

Monthly Review

New Left Notes

New Left Review

Our Generation

Radical America

Studies on the Left, 1959–67

8

Third world ideologies

Today there is considerable discussion of the split between the developed and developing nations or the rich and the poor nations that is not simply a reflection of nationalism or anticolonialism. The people of the Third World, called so because they are looking for a third route different from either capitalism or communism, see themselves as the exploited producers of the raw materials that other nations have used to develop their industrial systems and their wealth. They are also usually ex-colonies, nations that are basically suspicious of their old masters. Although control of such commodities as oil by a few countries sometimes gives the impression that the old relationship has changed significantly, it has not for most countries and the oil-producing countries feel that a higher price for oil is only just after years of exploitation.

This helps to explain the reasons for the desire to find a different position from capitalism, the excolonialists, or communism. Communism is often seen more favorably because of its lack of a colonial past, but it is still approached with caution. The struggle in the Third World to find a third position is one of the most important developments in the world today. If successful, there may be a significant change in world politics. If unsuccessful, the world may become embroiled in a war over the resources of the Third World countries.

Third World ideologies are not as coherent a set of beliefs and attitudes as are the other ideologies discussed here, but there are at least two central focuses—nonalignment and developmental socialism.

NONALIGNMENT

The term *neutralism* was the word used in the 1950s to describe the rejection by the Third World of both capitalism and communism and the position they took toward the so-called Cold War between the United States and the USSR. Since then the world has become more complicated and because of this the word *nonalignment* has replaced *neutralism* to suggest that these nations are not members of any power bloc. This is, of course, somewhat misleading since they now form a power bloc of their own.

The important point, though, is the rejection of the positions symbolized by the United States and the USSR and assertion that there is a better way, even if not yet entirely identified. Politically and economically it means that they will cooperate with any nation as it suits them.

The reasons for this are fairly obvious. In the first place, the colonial experience led to considerable distrust of many countries. Second, alignment with one bloc makes them an immediate target for another bloc. And third, they share many things in common, particularly poverty and a felt need for industrial development, that they don't share with the developed nations. This is, of course, especially true now that the growth of environmental concerns in countries like the United States and Canada conflict so strongly with the desire of the developing nations to develop their industries as rapidly and as cheaply as possible.

DEVELOPMENTAL SOCIALISM

Most of the new nations in the world label themselves *socialist,* but by that they mean a wide variety of things. Perhaps the only area in which there is complete agreement is in the rejection of capitalism, but even here there is a problem. The capitalism they reject is the traditional, completely laissez-faire capitalism that no longer exists. But the rejecting of capitalism, which leads to labeling diverse economic systems as *socialism*, is an important phenomenon whether or not capitalism is accurately perceived. The underlying reason for the antipathy to capitalism lies in the identification of capitalism with colonialism and neocolonialism. There is sufficient justification for such identification to develop a deep-rooted fear and rejection of the label *capitalism*, whatever the actual economic system may be. We have said that one of the reasons for the rejection of capitalism is the underlying rejection of the colonial system which was based on capitalism. Therefore, the result of this is simply that, given the major economic systems available in the modern world, the developing nations are most likely to accept socialism because it can be seen as a part of nationalism.

The most original development in socialism in the new nations, sometimes called African socialism but better called communalism or communitarian socialism, has been described best by Julius K. Nyerere (Tanzania), Leopold Senghor (Senegal), U Nu (Burma), and Vinoba Bhave (India). It stresses social solidarity and cooperation. A good illustration of the basic idea is found in the Swahili word that Nyerere uses for socialism, *ujamaa*—familyhood. As he puts it, "The foundation, and the objective, of African socialism is the extended family."[1] The extended family, the family that consists of a wide range of relatives that work cooperatively and share all the family resources, is the model for village and tribal socialism. The group owns the land, and the basic tools; the group works and shares as a family. All are fed, clothed, housed as the group can afford. The aged and the ill are supported. This form of socialism explicitly rejects the class divisions of communism. Here all are workers; there is little or no tradition of an exploiting class. Obviously there have been such exploiters but the supporters of communitarian socialism unanimously agree that the tradition which they are trying to revive was one of *ujamaa*.[2]

Obviously, there are serious problems in attempting to apply such a notion to the modern, industrial state that most leaders

---

[1] Julius K. Nyerere, "Ujamaa—The Basis of African Socialism" (1962), in *Ujamaa—Essays on Socialism* (New York: Oxford University Press, 1968), p. 11.

[2] See, for example, the essay by Ruth Shachter Morganthau, "African Socialism: Declaration of Ideological Independence," *Africa Report*, vol. 8 (May 1963), pp. 3–6.

in the new nations hope to develop, but there are also wide-spread attempts in the Western democracies to do the same thing in order to help overcome the isolation that so many people find in modern industrialized countries. This attempt can best be seen in the New Left.

COMMUNISM IN THE THIRD WORLD

Although Communism has not been adopted much among the developing countries, it has served as a model, particularly among Western revolutionaries. Only the developing Communist countries, such as China, Vietnam, North Korea, and Cuba have adopted this approach. In the other countries, it is represented by Communist political parties or other groups, such as national liberation movements, that are attempting to gain political power—so far they have been generally unsuccessful. This lack of success has a variety of causes, and assigning specific causes to specific cases would be foolhardy without a detailed analysis of all the factors involved, but it seems clear that one of the major reasons is the rejection of the Marxist–Leninist approach by most of the leaders of the developing nations.

The major point of interest in modern Marxist–Leninist socialism is found in the way it is being taken seriously by Western revolutionaries. Three men in particular, Mao Tse-tung, Ho Chi Minh, and Ernesto Che Guevara, are honored by Western revolutionaries. The three are symbols of the struggle against capitalism and Western imperialism and neocolonialism, and they are very important in this sense. Ho was a Vietnamese nationalist who successfully fought the West. "He has been too much the doer, the organizer, the conspirator, and, finally, the father of his own country to engage in the contemplation that serious writing generally requires."[3]

Che was the perfect archetype of the modern revolutionary. He was deeply concerned with the poverty he found throughout Central and South America, and he fought to improve

---

[3] Bernard B. Fall, "Ho Chi Minh—A Profile," in Fall, ed., *Ho Chi Minh on Revolution; Selected Writings, 1920–66* (New York: New American Library, 1967), p. v.

things. And whatever his motivation may have been, when one revolution was successfully completed, he joined another where he was killed. Young, intelligent, a fighter, and a martyr—there could be no better combination to impress young revolutionaries around the world.

Both Ho and Che are important symbols of nationalism and revolution. Mao is also a symbol in these senses, but in addition he led a successful developing country—the most populous in the world. Therefore, even though the leaders of the developing nations are not Communist, they view China and Mao with considerable interest, since they are more concerned with success than with form, and they hope to draw lessons from Mao.

Mao's importance is due to the success achieved in:

1. Winning a revolution.
2. Consolidating this revolution over a vast area and population.
3. Managing to feed this vast population better than previous regimes.
4. Beginning, with many setbacks, to industrialize.

Since these are the goals of both hopeful and successful revolutionary leaders, Mao was listened to.

CURRENT TRENDS

The Third World is currently undergoing a number of unusual strains both politically and economically that may have an effect on the ideologies, but at the moment they can only be noted. The most prominent recent event was the death of Mao Tse-tung, and it is simply too early to speak with any certainty about its effects. The conflicts within Africa are growing rapidly. In South Africa and Rhodesia, black majorities are fighting the ruling white minority with growing vigor. In the rest of sub-Saharan Africa conflict among the various nations is growing, particularly in light of the erratic activities of Idi Amin in Uganda and strained relations between Tanzania and Zambia. Finally, the civil war in Angola led to significant armed interference from outside Africa, particularly from Cuba and

included the continuing involvement of white mercenary sol-
diers, usually on the side of the ex-colonial power.

Economically, the rising price of oil has effected most of the
Third World much more than it has effected the developed
countries. The Third World has had to pay higher prices both
for the fuel to feed its beginning industries and for the products it imports. These countries are not in a position to make
significant adjustments in their economies and the prices of
the raw materials they export have tended to stay relatively low.

It is difficult to see the effect of all this on the ideologies,
but the growing violence may reflect a frustration at the failure
to develop as rapidly as desired and particularly a frustration
due to the fact that so many of the events that retard development are completely out of their control.

Another aspect of this frustration is the growth of organized
terrorism around the world. Much of the terrorism is related
to specific issues in the Third World, particularly in the Middle
East and is caused by the almost 30-year conflict over Israel.
But the important point is not the specific excuse for terrorism
but the seemingly growing belief that there is no hope for
solutions to a variety of problems by nonviolent means.

SUGGESTED READINGS

Alpert, Paul. *Partnership or Confrontation? Poor Lands and Rich.*
   New York: Free Press, 1973.

Anderson, Charles W.; von der Mehden, Fred R.; and Young, Craw-
   ford. *Issues of Political Development.* Englewood Cliffs, N.J.:
   Prentice-Hall, 1967.

Bâ, Sylvia Washington. *The Concept of Negritude in the Poetry of
   Leopold Sedar Senghor.* Princeton, N.J.: Princeton University
   Press, 1973.

Brockway, Fenner. *African Socialism; A Background Book.* Chester
   Springs, Pa.: Dufour Editions, 1963.

Desfosses, Helen, and Levesque, Jacques, eds. *Socialism in the Third
   World.* New York: Praeger, 1975.

Fall, Bernard B., ed. *Ho Chi Minh on Revolution; Selected Writings,
   1920–66.* New York: New American Library, 1967.

Fanon, Frantz. *Toward the African Revolution (Political Essays).* Trans.
   Haskon Chevalier. New York: Grove Press, 1967.

Friedland, William H., and Rosberg, Carl G., eds. *African Socialism*. Stanford, Calif.: Stanford University Press, 1964.

Gerassi, John, ed. *Venceremos! The Speeches and Writings of Ernesto Che Guevara*. New York: Simon & Schuster, 1968.

Goldthorpe, J. E. *The Sociology of the Third World; Disparity and Involvement*. Cambridge, Eng.: Cambridge University Press, 1975.

Guevara, Ernesto Che. *Reminiscenses of the Cuban Revolutionary War*. Trans. Victoria Ortiz. New York: Monthly Review Press, 1968.

————. *Socialism and Man*. New York: Young Socialist Alliance, 1969.

Horowitz, Irving Louis; De Castro, Josue; and Gerassi, John, eds. *Latin American Radicalism: A Documentary Report on Left and Nationalist Movements*. New York: Random House, 1969.

Inkeles, Alex, and Smith, David H. *Becoming Modern; Individual Change in Six Developing Countries*. Cambridge, Mass.: Harvard University Press, 1974.

Johnson, Dale, ed. *The Chilean Road to Socialism*. Garden City: Anchor Books, 1973.

Kilson, Martin, ed. *New States in the Modern World*. Cambridge, Mass.: Harvard University Press, 1975.

Legum, Colin. *Pan-Africanism*. New York: Frederick A. Praeger, 1965.

Leys, Colin, ed. *Politics and Change in Developing Countries; Studies in the Theory and Practice of Development*. Cambridge, Eng.: Cambridge University Press, 1969.

Markovitz, Irving Leonard, ed. *African Politics and Society; Basic Issues and Problems of Government and Development*. New York: Free Press, 1970.

Nasser, Gamal Abdel. *The Philosophy of the Revolution*. Buffalo, N.Y.: Smith, Keynes & Marshall, 1959.

Nyerere, Julius K. *Freedom and Socialism; Uhuru na Ujamaa, A Selection from Writings and Speeches 1965–1970*. Dar es Salaam: Oxford University Press, 1968.

————. *Freedom and Development. Uhuru na Maendelo; A Selection of Writings and Speeches 1968–1973*. Dar es Salaam: Oxford University Press, 1973.

Sayegh, Fayez A., ed. *The Dynamics of Neutralism in the Arab World: A Symposium*. San Francisco: Chandler Publishing Co., 1964.

Schapera, I. *Government and Politics in Tribal Society*. New York: Frederick A. Praeger, 1964.

Senghor, Leopold Sedar. *On African Socialism*. New York: Frederick A. Praeger, 1964.

Shaffer, Harry G., and Prybyla, Jan E., eds. *From Underdevelopment* to *Affluence; Western, Soviet, and Chinese Views.* New York: Appleton-Century-Crofts, 1968.

Sigmund, Paul E., ed.   *The Ideologies of the Developing Nations.* New York: Frederick A. Praeger, 1967.

Tullis, F. La Mond.   *Politics and Social Change in Third World Countries.* N.Y.: John Wiley and Sons, 1973.

Von der Mehden, Fred R.   *Politics of the Developing Nations.* 2d ed. Englewood Cliffs, N.J.: Prentice-Hall, 1969.

Zeitlin, Maurice.   *Revolutionary Politics and the Cuban Working Class.* New York: Harper & Row, 1970.

9

Conclusion

We have dealt with a number of sets of ideologies in this book. It is important to note that each is a set of ideologies and not in any case a monolithic position free of disagreements. We have indicated major disagreements and differences of opinion in connection with all of them. I have attempted in this final chapter to compare these ideologies with regard to two sets of categories—one directed at questions of political philosophy (see the questions in Chapter 1), the other directed at the various parts of the social system. A comparison has to be very general, while attempting to avoid being too broad and therefore meaningless, and obviously a number of points will only be relevant to certain ideologies.

The first question concerns human nature, and thus we ask: (1) what are the basic characteristics of humans as humans, and (2) what effect does the nature of humanity have upon the political system? The first question is answered in surprisingly similar ways by all of the ideologies with the exception of fascism and national socialism. Communism, democracy, anarchism, and the New Left argue that the human being is fundamentally capable of a high degree of community spirit and good feeling toward other humans. Fascism and national socialism stress the factors of hate and fear rather than the good in people. There is also underlying much of communism, democracy, and anarchism a belief that humans are fundamentally rational. Nationalism, fascism, and national socialism do not stress our rationality to the extent that the other ideologies do. Fascism and national socialism clearly stress our irrational side. The New Left attempts to recognize both sides. Nationalism stresses the emotional, not specifically the irrational, characteristics of humanity.

The second question, What effect does the nature of humanity have upon the political system?, is not answered directly or conclusively by most of the ideologies. For communism, fascism, national socialism, anarchism, and the New Left the concern is mostly with the effect that changes in the political system have on people. This is most obvious in anarchism with its stress on the development of a noncoercive society that will allow for the growth of a better, more sociable human being. Democracy has perhaps the most sophisticated approach. The whole complex of ideas focusing on freedom with limits, representation with regular checks by voters, and general equality are based on the position that each individual is capable of both high-minded self-sacrifice and corruption, that the human is an extremely complex creature that cannot be encompassed by a unidimensional system.

The second set of questions, the origin of society and government or the state, are on the whole, ignored. We have indicated at places that both traditional Marxism and certain arguments for democracy do talk about these origins, but again contemporary political ideologies are not very often concerned with such questions. Ideologies today are not concerned with these questions for the simple reason that many people view them as irrelevant. People everywhere find themselves in society and ruled by government, and therefore the question of how this happened does not seem to be very important.

Anarchism, because it rejects the notion of government and the state, does deal with their origins. Generally, the conclusion is that humans at some time or other formed a society for protection. Some anarchists argue that government was also formed out of society for protection or security. Others argue that government came about simply by usurpation on the part of some group within society. The reasoning behind both arguments is that each tends to accept society as a necessary form of cooperation, whereas government is rejected as not necessary. It can and should be done away with because it stifles our ability to cooperate with one another.

Questions in the third set, centering on political obligation, are answered by all the ideologies, but in some, such as democracy, the answers are so diverse and so varied that it is difficult even to summarize them. Why does or should humans obey the government or, in order to include anarchism, should they at all? The simplest answer is of course given by anarchism. There is no reason why they should obey government.

For fascism and national socialism, government must be obeyed because it is the government—because the system of leadership demands obedience. People must obey because it is their role to obey and to be led. Communism would argue that the dictatorship of the proletariat should be obeyed because it provides security and economic benefits in the period of transition from bourgeois society to a Full Communist society. At the same time, the individual living under the capitalist society has no specific obligation to obey that society. As a matter of fact, the ideology implies that the proletariat has a specific obligation to attempt to overthrow the government. This is not as true in contemporary communism as it was in early Communist doctrine. It would probably be more accurate to say today that a member of the proletariat in a bourgeois or capitalist society neither has a specific obligation to obey or to attempt to overthrow that government.

Democracy is a much more complicated problem because of the wide variety of reasons given for justifying obedience, some of which are similar to the reasons given in other ideologies. These reasons may be summarized somewhat as follows: (1) security, (2) other benefits, (3) requirement by the community justifying obedience itself, and (4) because it is within the power of the citizen to change the entire system while still obeying. Democracy raises other problems with regard to revolution and the possibility of disobedience. Contemporary democratic theory is beginning to accept the idea of disobedience without revolution (this was discussed in Chapter 3 on democracy). Most democratic ideology rejects revolution within a democracy because of reason (4) for obedience given above. As we saw in the New Left, there is a basic disagreement over the question of violence, but there is an acceptance of disobedience and revolution.

The fourth set of questions concerns liberty. Communism would argue that under Full Communism the individual is given complete liberty. Under the dictatorship of the proletariat, the individual must have sharply curtailed liberty in order to achieve the transition. Fascism and national socialism would essentially consider the question of liberty irrelevant. The individual's freedom, such as it is, is found entirely in giving himself or herself up to the state. Anarchism, since there is no government, has a system of complete liberty. The New Left comes closest to anarchism. Democracy again is the most complicated of the ideologies. Democracy contends that it provides for liberty within the system, but at the same time, liberty must exist in a limited way; the problem for the democratic system is to maintain a system in which the people of the country are willing and able to limit themselves, both individually and through the legal system, so that the liberty of one individual does not, in fact, infringe upon the liberty of another.

The fifth set of questions concerns equality. Clearly fascism and national socialism reject any form of equality. Anarchism generally considers that all individuals must be considered to be equal socially and politically. There is considerable debate among anarchists whether or not economic equality is a worthwhile goal. Communism stresses social equality and includes political equality in the ideal of Full Communism. In the period of the dictatorship of the proletariat, social equality would exist, but political equality would not, because of the necessity of strong power at the top. Economic equality is a goal of communism except that it does not argue for complete economic equality. It argues for an overcoming of the extremes of economic inequality. This last point would hold true equally well for many democratic theories, including both democratic capitalism and democratic socialism, the difference between the two being primarily those of means rather than of ends. Democracy stresses political and legal equality and the equality of opportunity. It is not as concerned with economic equality as with the other forms of equality. The New Left is different only in its emphasis on social equality.

The sixth set of questions concerns the problem of community. We have stressed that for nationalism, developmental socialism, and the New Left, community is a major concern. For the other ideologies, this point is not as significant, although the notion of the nation or the race in fascism and national socialism has elements of the idea of community within it. The other ideologies tend to accept an idea of community as a goal and are concerned with how one achieves it but are not very conclusive in their answers. The New Left is fundamentally concerned with the question of a community. It believes that one of the most important things that must be done in contemporary society is to redevelop this sense of community that has disappeared with modern industrialization and specialization.

The seventh set of questions relates to power. Power for the Communist ideology varies depending on whether you are concerned with the dictatorship of the proletariat or Full Communism. In Full Communism, power would be widely diversified among all individuals. In the dictatorship of the proletariat, power, in fact, rests in the hands of a few at the very top of the Communist party. Some contend that power resides in the party as such, but it would be more accurate to see it in the hands of a few. Fascism and national socialism also invest power in the hands of the very few or one individual at the very top. Democracy argues that power is diversified among all individuals. It would be more accurate to see it in the hands of those actively concerned with the governmental process and actively working within it. There is no focus of power in anarchism; power is centered in each individual separately. In the New Left, power centers in the community.

The next two sets of questions, justice and the end of society or government, may be conveniently collapsed together because each of the ideologies would contend that justice will be found by achieving the end of the ideology or the ends of the society or government. For communism, justice is found in the proletariat owning the means of production and distribution. For the democrat, justice is found in the individual citizen controlling his or her own destiny through the political system. In even stronger terms, this is true for the New Left. For the Fascist and National Socialist, justice is found in the individual giving himself or herself up willingly and thoroughly to the state. For the anarchist, justice is found in the end of government and the achievement of a society based on the individual.

The final set of questions concerns the structural characteristics of government. Clearly, this is irrelevant to nationalism, anarchism, Full Communism, and the New Left. The others do not consistently answer the question in a way that makes valid generalizations possible.

In the answers to these questions, we are able to see the positions of the ideologies toward the fundamental political questions. We note that the answers vary considerably from ideology to ideology but also that the answers are sometimes quite divergent within a given ideology. This overview gives us some basis of comparison of the political aspects of the ideologies. In order to fully understand the value system of the ideology, we must look at certain other social institutions. Therefore, a second stage of comparison of the ideologies must look at these other subsystems of the social system.

The first is the social stratification and mobility system. Communism argues that there will be no social stratification and hence no social mobility system within Full Communism. Under the dictatorship of the proletariat, the only stratification system that should exist would be that between the proletariat and the remnants of the bourgeoisie and the peasantry. The only form of mobility that would be possible would be for the bourgeoisie and the peasantry to move into the proletariat. In fact, the dictatorship of the proletariat has produced a new social stratification system which establishes a class of technocrats who essentially operate the government, the Communist party, and the various important institutions of the country. Therefore, the Communist social stratification system is based in large part upon two factors: (1) membership in the Communist party, and (2) education.

The democratic social stratification and mobility system is based primarily on money and education. Democratic countries tend to view their stratification systems in purely economic terms, with some questions about certain relatively low-paid professional groups such as college professors and high school teachers. The primary means of mobility in the democratic system is education. As we noticed in discussing the New Left, its main concern with the social stratification and mobility system is that each individual must be capable of mobility. There is not any defined system by which mobility can be achieved. The New Left rejects any stratification system as being irrelevant, even though it accepts the idea of there being some differences among individuals within society. For fascism and national socialism, stratification is based on race, indications of loyalty to the nation, service in the party, and service to the state. Mobility is based on the same standards. For anarchism, there would be no social stratification system and hence no mobility system.

The socialization system is made up of various institutions in society that help to give to an individual the values of that society. The primary institutions of socialization are the family, the educational system, the religious system, and, in modern societies, the mass media. Children gain ideas about the life around them before they are capable of articulating those ideas themselves. They hear their parents give positive or negative connotations to certain words and phrases that the children can identify but for which they have no meaning. For example, a child in the United States might gain a positive connotation with the word *democratic* and a negative connotation with the word *republican* from parents that were strongly in favor of the Democratic party. The child continues throughout life hearing various words given particular connotations.

Again, in the United States as an example, the child might very often hear the word *communism* connected with the idea of evil or something bad. Therefore, before the individual is at all capable of understanding what communism is about, he or she is convinced that it is bad, and this type of connotation is extremely difficult to change. Therefore, these institutions of socialization are extremely important if a society is going to be able to imbue individuals with the values of the system. Thus, it is instructive to look at some of the attitudes of these ideologies toward the major institutions of socialization.

It is noteworthy, first, that communism, fascism, and national socialism almost without exception, hold that the mass media must be carefully controlled so that it will present a picture of the system to the public that has positive connotations. Anarchism and the New Left tend to argue for a completely unlimited mass media. Democracy comes very close to this, only limiting the media in cases of libel and only in relatively rare cases. Democracies have found a greater problem, though, in connection with the unwillingness of governmental officials to give the mass media complete information, thus, in a sense, controlling the media.

One would think that communism, fascism, and national socialism would also argue for control of the other institutions of socialization, and in some cases they do. Communism clearly argues for a great control of religion because it is seen as a direct threat to the ideology. Fascism and national socialism tended, on the other hand, to view religion as a positive support of the nationalism that was so important to the ideology, and in many cases, the religious system did, in fact, support fascism and national socialism, or at least did not oppose it very actively. Neither anarchism, democracy, nor the New Left is concerned with controlling religion, although in anarchism one often finds an antipathy toward religion. Many anarchists believe that religion consistently supports the state and thus is opposed to the anarchist philosophy. Most, but not all, democratic ideologies and democratic systems argue for a separation between the religious system and the political system, but they also seem to believe that religion can be a positive support for the political system of democracy.

Every ideology is concerned with using the educational system as a direct support for the ideology. All of the ideologies believe that the educational system is the most potent force of socialization within the social system and believe that the educational system must be used to support the values of the society or the ideology. On the other hand, none of the ideologies, with the partial exceptions of anarchism and the New Left, says much about changing the family system in such a way that it might bring about support for the ideology. Attempts have been made in some Communist countries to bring about such changes, but they have so far been unsuccessful. It is probably better policy to attempt to imbue the parents with the values that one wishes to have passed on to the children and if the parents do, in fact, accept the values, they will be automatically passed on to the children. Therefore, it is not really necessary to tamper with the family system.

In each of the ideologies that we have discussed, a considerable amount of time has been spent analyzing the last aspect of the social system, the economic system. It is not necessary here to repeat those arguments. It is only necessary to say that each of the ideologies has differing attitudes toward the economic system. Communism has combined with an authoritarian political system a state socialist economic system. Democracy has combined with its political system either a capitalist form of economic system or a socialist one. Fascism and national socialism have authoritarian political systems combined with slightly modified capitalist systems. Developmental socialism is connected to a wide variety of political systems. Anarchism, we indicated, was unclear concerning the appropriate economic system for its political, or one might better say, its apolitical system. The New Left accepts democratic socialism.

These comments have been very general, but hopefully they provide some basis for comparison among the ideologies. It is important for a student of contemporary political ideologies to understand both the similarities and the differences among these ideologies. We do not know what the future holds in store for any of these, but it is important for us to understand what each of these ideologies accepts so that we will be able to evaluate them objectively.

In conclusion, it is hoped that the reader will reflect carefully on the challenges that the variety of belief systems poses for his or her belief system. What can be expected of humanity in the future? Are we rational, capable of determining on a desirable future and working for it or are we irrational, incapable of so choosing, or unwilling to work for our goal? Must humans be coerced or can we cooperate without coercion? Can humanity achieve a meaningful equality or is equality of any sort an impossible dream? Can humans be free or is freedom a dangerous fantasy? All these questions, and many others, will be answered in the near future. We must reflect on the society in which we want to live. We must ask ourselves, in what ways are we affected by ideologies? Do we have an ideology? What are its elements? How does it affect us? How do the ideologies held by others affect us? The answers to all these questions will affect the way we spend our lives.

Index

This book has been set in 10 point Optima, leaded 3 points, and 9 point Optima, leaded 2 points. Chapter numbers are 48 point Americana and chapter titles are 24 point Americana. The size of the type page is 24 picas by 45 picas.